BREAKING FREE

glimpses of a Buddhist life

SRIMALA

BREAKING FREE

glimpses of a Buddhist life

WINDHORSE PUBLICATIONS

Published by Windhorse Publications
Unit 1-316 The Custard Factory
Gibb Street
Birmingham
B9 4AA

Printed by Biddles Ltd, Walnut Tree House,
Woodbridge Park, Guildford, Surrey, GU1 1DA

Design: Graham Parker
Cover design: Dhammarati
Cover illustration: Alison Harper

Cover photographs show Srimala with Sona and their children in 1976,
and Srimala with Ratnasuri and Sanghadevi in 1989

British Library Cataloguing in Publication Data
A catalogue record for this book is available from the British Library

ISBN 1 899579 03 6

PUBLISHER'S NOTE: Since this work is intended for a general readership, Pali and Sanskrit
words have been transliterated without the diacritical marks that would have been
appropriate in a work of a more scholarly nature.

The quotations that start each section come from the Dhammapada,
a renowned early Buddhist scripture.
The translation used here is by Thomas Byrom in
Shambhala's Pocket Classics series.

Contents

Editor's Preface

In a small hut by a waterfall, in the depths of a Scottish winter, I sat opposite a woman whose radiant calmness and strength quieted my trembling. I took a deep breath and we began the ceremony which was to change my life for ever: ancient words to mark the beginning of a new life. In just a few minutes it was done. I was now a member of the Western Buddhist Order, committed with body, speech, and mind to the Buddha's path to Enlightenment.

Ever since the ordination of Mahaprajapati, the Buddha's aunt, more than two thousand five hundred years ago, women have been making that commitment; for a woman to be ordained within the Buddhist tradition is to follow an ancient lineage. But in this century, in the West, something new has emerged: the ordination of women by women.

Srimala was one of the first women in the Western Buddhist Order to become a preceptor, one who performs the ordination of others. By the time of my ordination in 1993, she had herself been ordained for eighteen years, and there were more than a hundred women in the women's wing of the Western Buddhist Order. At the time of my ordination, and in the years leading up to it, I came to know her as a deeply peaceful woman, almost dauntingly so. I was struck by her consistency: her calmness, her unshakability, her kind but uncompromising questioning of aspects of my spiritual practice as I worked towards ordination.

Having come to appreciate Srimala for these qualities, I have appreciated them all the more in working with her on this book, and realizing afresh the tremendous effort she has made to develop them. The story she tells here is of her gradual, even painful emergence from shy and awkward beginnings; the balancing act of honouring her commitment to bringing up her children and at the same time deepening her involvement in her own spiritual journey and that of other women; and the struggle to shake off dependence on sexual partners.

Anyone coming across the Friends of the Western Buddhist Order today encounters a whole world of possibilities. Order members teach meditation in many of the world's cities, hold retreats at country retreat centres, run businesses based on the Buddhist principles of Right Livelihood, live in communities dedicated to the shared practice of the Buddha's teachings. But when Srimala went along to her first meditation class in the early seventies, there was just one FWBO centre, in London, and it was run by the movement's founder, the Venerable Sangharakshita.

By his own account, Sangharakshita's return to England after twenty years in India was a culture shock, to say the least. He had left war-time London as an army conscript bound for India; he returned, a Buddhist monk highly respected for his years of scholarship and experience, to the now legendary London of the swinging sixties. Undaunted, he set about establishing the new Buddhist movement he could see was needed, in the prevailing atmosphere of LSD, love-ins, and the Rolling Stones.

The FWBO as Srimala first encountered it was a very young movement, and it had all the zeal, exuberance, and naïvety of youth. New ideas of how to live, how to relate to others, how to be a Buddhist with all one's heart and soul, were seized upon and put into practice without hesitation. As a young mother Srimala was confronted with radical changes of life-style as she and her husband plunged into the experimentation and chaos of those times.

Today, almost thirty years after it was founded, the FWBO is, in a sense, more established. The maturity of the spiritual practice of Order members like Srimala who have been ordained for more than twenty years is reflected in the greater maturity of the Buddhist movement they have dedicated their lives to creating—although in the context of the whole Buddhist tradition, a few decades' experience is really no more than a beginning. Perhaps the most significant development in the history of the FWBO so far is the fact that Sangharakshita, now seventy, has been able to hand on the responsibility for ordaining others which is at the heart of the continuing life of any Buddhist movement.

But the fact that this new Buddhist movement is now not quite so new, has perhaps even come of age, does not mean—*must* not mean —that it has settled down. The authentic Buddhist life will always be an utterly radical one, and people choosing to follow it and committing themselves to it today come up against just the same issues faced by Srimala and the others involved in the revolutionary early days. How do we want to live? Can we contemplate a life without the apparent security of living with a sexual partner? Do we want children? If we do, or if we have them already, how are we to combine bringing them up well with our spiritual aspirations? How much of our lives are we prepared to share with our friends? How far will we allow ourselves to go in embracing a way of life dedicated to the attainment of Enlightenment?

These are not easy questions, and in writing this book Srimala has not made light of them—while at the same time she is able to see the funny side of the predicaments she finds herself in. It is typical of her that in writing the story of her spiritual life she has focused on the doubts and difficulties more than the achievement of overcoming them—typical because her particular combination of shyness and determination has developed into a quiet confidence that allows her to be fearlessly honest. The writing of this book is another step forward in that process. Her story shows that with determination—which she has clearly possessed throughout her life—an extraordinary life can emerge from the most ordinary of circumstances.

When I asked Sangharakshita what he remembered about Srimala from the early days, he recalled how as a new Order member she used to come along to a class for people who wanted to practise giving talks on Buddhism. You could attend this class on one condition: you had to stand up and give a talk. Not the first time you came, or the second, but certainly the third, you would have to address the others present, and give a short talk on some aspect of the Dharma. Although Srimala was very shy and nervous, she managed to give her talk. Sangharakshita remembers that as a particular turning point in the growth of Srimala's confidence.

These days word of mouth is not enough to keep those involved in the FWBO in touch with events; among various media of communication, a regular FWBO video newsreel lets people know what's going on at Buddhist centres throughout the world. A recent newsreel showed the ordination of seven women into the Order in India. For women to be ordained in India involves a tremendous overcoming of conditions and circumstances. On this occasion a crowd of thousands was present to witness the public ordination of the new Order members. As each woman went forward to receive the kesa which would symbolize the commitment she had made, clapping and cheering echoed and re-echoed in acknowledgement of the step being taken. And the woman sitting next to the shrine, in front of that great throng of people, looking unruffled and completely at home as she welcomed each of the new Dharmacharinis into the Order, was Srimala.

Vidyadevi

Those who awaken
Never rest in one place.
Like swans, they rise
And leave the lake.

On the air they rise
And fly an invisible course,
Gathering nothing, storing nothing.
Their food is knowledge.
They live upon emptiness.
They have seen how to break free.

Introduction

I am the youngest of my mother's three children and the third of my father's five. My parents divorced when I was about three years old. My brother, my two half-sisters, and I have all become Buddhists, involved in the Friends of the Western Buddhist Order.

I was, on the whole, a quiet, shy, introverted child, but occasionally I would assert myself. At my secondary school we had to choose between Latin, domestic science, and woodwork or metalwork. Two years previously a boy had taken up domestic science but it appeared to be unheard of for girls to take up woodwork—and that's what I wanted to do. I was warned that the course would be far more technical than just banging bits of wood together, and I was a little daunted by what looked to me like a maths lesson going on in the metalwork room. But what daunted me most was the fact that I would be the only girl in the class. My determination kept me going right up to the very first lesson. I hardly took in a word of what the teacher said as he showed us around the workshop. My heart was pounding away and I began to feel faint. I excused myself and I'm afraid I never went back. I quite enjoyed domestic science though; I made a good pineapple upside-down cake and I learnt to make clothes.

When I was sixteen I fell in love with a French boy. With little motivation to pursue my A-level studies I decided, unbeknown to him, that I would go and live with him in Montpellier where he was at university, and we would probably get married. But rather than encouraging me in my romantic dream (I hadn't been able to imagine what on earth I would do while he was studying) he seemed to be losing interest. One morning I received a letter indicating that it was all over. I had latched on to him as someone who would save me from a miserable, pointless existence, and now I was on my own again. I couldn't go off to school as though everything was normal. And I couldn't just stay at home to pine and await my mother's return from work. My distress was serious— I had to do something. Where could I go? My sister was at college in Staffordshire. I had no money for a train. I would simply have to throw caution to the wind and hitch-hike up there. It was a daring and foolhardy thing to do but I was glad that I'd done it and I was cheered up a bit by Joanna and her high-spirited college friends.

Reluctantly I decided to carry on at school. I didn't know what else to do. I felt like a rebel without a cause. I wanted to be a drop-out but I didn't know what or where to drop out to. I came from a family of teachers. I identified strongly with my mother and from an early age had assumed that I would be an English teacher like her. Now, with no other ideas before me, I applied to do a course in teacher training. I was surprised and rather humiliated when the rejections came pouring in and I was only offered a place at a college I hadn't even applied to. It was 1969, the hippie era, and having heard about communes in America I thought maybe I'd go and live in one. But I couldn't just go off on my own, so I looked in the paper at advertisements for `3rd girl to share flat'. I wanted to leave home but I found I couldn't do it without something more tangible to go towards. Then Ray asked me to marry him. He was like an anchor securing himself to me. I felt stabilized and life seemed to make more sense. Perhaps after all I would lead a more or less conventional life, with a man on whom I could depend.

I conceived my first child not long after being introduced to the Friends of the Western Buddhist Order. I was ordained into the Order in 1975 while pregnant with my second child. We were by then living a far from conventional life.

Ray and I had married and started a family, but we had also become interested in Buddhism. We soon found that we couldn't simply add a touch of Buddhism to our normal lives. If we were seriously interested then the Dharma, the teaching of the Buddha, the Truth, would need to be at the very centre of our existence; or at least we would be trying to lead our lives from that basis.

Having thought that marriage and dependence on one another was what we wanted, we came across an Ideal that was in a sense to destroy the new family unit that we had begun to construct. Possibilities of what life had in store opened up before us. People were talking of 'getting into a rut' and of wanting to `leave the rat-race'. The popular escape at the time was to go back to Nature, to live in the country growing vegetables. We had discovered a path that was far more radical. If we weren't satisfied with an ordinary life we needn't be: we could free ourselves from it. But on this path there were no half measures; if we wanted to escape the greed, pain, and confusion, the rut of ordinary existence, we must aim to escape from the endless rounds of birth and death, we must escape from the

Wheel of Life and aim for Enlightenment. If we turned away from the world and all its mundane values we could turn towards real freedom and the most precious life imaginable. We could transform ourselves. The rebel in me had found a cause, and the drop-out a direction.

Despite the many positive aspects of family life, it is the antithesis to the spiritual life because it has a basically selfish intention. It can provide a supportive environment for human growth, encouraging regard for others and the taking on of responsibility, but the basis for this potential is not disinterested love. The family is based on attachment, which from a Buddhist perspective inevitably leads to suffering. It engenders possessiveness, selfishness, greed, jealousy, even hatred, and it encourages a false sense of having, of belonging, of security, and of well-being. It did not therefore provide us with the easiest of conditions from which to reorientate our lives, but it was our working ground. We set about trying to free ourselves from its strong, habitual hold in as responsible a way as our youthful naïvety would allow. Perhaps the most significant step we took was in deciding to live separately.

For twenty years I often felt as though I was living in two conflicting worlds. One foot was firmly embedded in the mundane world, where I had my responsibilities as a mother, and my home and children to attend to. The other foot was set on the spiritual path; I was trying to develop as an individual, trying to deepen a sense of solidarity with all other living beings, trying to break free of identification with, and immersion in, the roles of wife and mother, trying to fathom what life was *really* all about. For much of the time I felt held back in my efforts to develop, experiencing limitations which would remain with me until my daughters had flown the nest. I would mark off time in two-year blocks, looking ahead to the next slightly more freed-up stage: the end of nappies, the start of school, able to make their own lunch box, travel alone, do without a baby-sitter.... At other times I looked more positively on my life-style and my own particular circumstances. I appreciated not being in the position that some of my friends were in; having already embarked on the spiritual life they were now agonizing over the question of whether or not to have children. I sometimes complained but I don't think I ever really regretted having them. Although having children has not been the major preoccupation of my life—dominant though it was for twenty years—it did to some extent satisfy me. I did what my woman's body wanted to do. In many respects I appreciated having the definite framework of being a mother. I had a tangible job to do. If I wanted to do that job at all well and if I wanted to be more than a mother, I had to be disciplined. The framework of my domestic responsibilities pro-vided me with a structure in which I could work consciously on becoming more aware, more emotionally positive, and within which I would do whatever I could to help with the running of Buddhist activities. I found that the limitations I experienced could not all be attributed to my situation and that in itself it afforded me plenty of scope for spiritual practice. All too easily I could take my frustration out on my exuberant but innocent daughters, flaring up at them in unreasonable anger. But how unfair, unkind, and unsatisfactory. When I saw what I was doing, I was forced to seek deeper communi-cation with spiritual friends.

I had always imagined that life as a mother would get easier as each two years passed by. But it didn't—it was just different. When my youngest daughter began her A-level course I hardly dared tempt fate by declaring that I had arrived at what should have been my last two-year stint. A friend had warned me not to think in terms of a specific time when I would be free to walk out of the door, all my parental responsibilities having been fulfilled. And so I turned my attention to a gradual approach to leaving home. I knew that after all those years it would not be an easy task. In spite of the limitations I'd felt, and still hounded by the noisy, trivial emotional life of teenage girls, this was home and I was used to living with my daughters. As they grew up we seemed to grow closer in a genuine way rather than simply being bound together by an umbilical cord. And so my attachment to them had deepened.

It dawned on me that the warning I had been given was not al-together valid. So long as I had a daughter alive I would be a mother. However, if I played my cards right I saw no reason why I couldn't set a date for my official `leaving home'. My cards came up trumps and so, almost twenty-one years after conceiving my first child, I drove off to spend a year, more or less alone, in France.

It had seemed to me desirable, even necessary, to do something spe-cific to mark the transition from being needed at home, from being bound up with domestic responsibilities, to being free to step into a life-style more conducive to my spiritual endeavours. I wanted sym-bolically to cut the umbilical cord. I wanted to leave my daughters to fend for themselves. They could cook adequately, but would they sur-vive without me to remove mosquitoes and wasps and to comfort them on their sick-beds?

I wanted to take some time away from all of my usual respon-sibilities. I wanted to look back on the last phase of my life, the last twenty-one years. I wanted to consider what I had been doing. I wanted to get a clearer, more objective perspective on it all. I wanted to identify just where the struggles of my life had led me. I was aware that there were certain interweaving threads running through my life. If I looked back, might I detect the emergence of a distinct pattern? Perhaps, if I were no longer so bound up in my life, I might be able to build more boldly on to that pattern. I wanted to look at the past and let it go, let go especially of the mother in me, in order that I might continue even more wholeheartedly on my way to becoming truly human, and beyond. I wanted to tell the story of my journey from home towards homelessness.

It wasn't enough for me to ponder on my story and to tell it, as it were, to myself. Being of a shy, withdrawing nature I have experienced a considerable lack of ease, over the years, in articulating my thoughts and feelings. Having been encouraged to view writing as a spiritual practice I have come to appreciate its value as a means of clarifying and communicating my experience. I decided therefore to write up my story, to bring my experience out into the open and offer it to a wider audience. I hope it will be of benefit to others as well as to myself.

I imagine my audience will be mainly women. But not, I hope, exclusively so.

I want in particular to address my daughters, Shanti and Sundari, without whom there might have been no story. I want to give them a broader view of their mother and, I hope, some idea of what being a Buddhist means to me. I know they have at times thought that I was a bit weird and ascribed it all, lock, stock, and barrel, to my being Buddhist. They have grown up into delightful young women, proving, I like to think, the success of their unconventionally `broken' home which they sometimes found difficult to make sense of. I hope my story will help them to understand their parents' peculiar ways, although I'm nervously prepared for it to add to their bewilderment.

I am writing for my mother. Although I don't tell her much about what I do, I believe she appreciates that I am following a worthwhile path. I would like to spell out to her why I chose to step out of marriage. I offer my story to her in appreciation of the example she set me. I never became an English teacher but I have built on the encouragement she gave me at an early age to value the art of writing.

I would like my sister, Joanna, to understand something of what I have been doing all these years. We grew up together, but gradually we went our separate ways. She followed through her teaching career and made a good job of it. She too thinks I'm weird. She has always been such a good auntie to my daughters, showing them the ways of the world in a way that their retiring mother couldn't have done. I am indebted to her.

To Sinhadevi, who made my dreams of friendship come true, I offer this story.

To the friends who want to know more about my life, I offer this story.

To other mothers and those considering that way of life, I offer this story in the hope that it will be encouraging. I have written predominantly of my struggles, but I hope I have shown that they were not in vain.

To my father, who perhaps thinks I am a bit of a lost cause—at least in a worldly sense—I offer what I have written, with thanks for his encouraging me not to fear the unconventional, and kindly giving me the use of his cottage in France in which to write.

I hope Lokamitra, my brother, will be interested too. It is him I have to thank for pointing my quietly questioning heart in the right direction.

I know that Sona, my ex-husband and dear friend, is interested. I consider my story to show the real success of our marriage.

Without Subhuti, I doubt that I would have written this story. I offer it to him by way of saying thank you for his encouragement, insistence, and most of all, his friendship.

Sangharakshita, my treasured teacher, Bhante, knows the gist of my story. Many times I have wondered whether I had bitten off more than I could chew. I could readily appreciate the traditional Buddhist point of view that as regards following the spiritual life men, generally speaking, have a head start over women. However, whatever limitations and disadvantages I encountered, I was always reassured by Bhante that they need not throw me off course, that I need not allow them to deter me from my spiritual aspiration. Without him I would probably be living a wet and miserable life in Wales. I hope that I will always be guided by him. With deepest gratitude and love I offer the written version of my story to him in the hope that it will afford him a few laughs and thereby a longer life.

This story is my story. It is written from my own subjective viewpoint. I have not tried to give an objectively accurate account of the experiences and incidents I have described. Sometimes my memory served me well, sometimes it didn't. Other people involved in my story might well remember their own parts in a very different light—I ask them to bear with me.

My story is a personal exploration of the interplay between love, attachment, and suffering, and the tension experienced whilst living a householder's life and trying to lead a spiritual one. In the course of telling it I have referred to some Buddhist terms which will be explained in the glossary. I have also made some connections which, on reading, will not necessarily be obvious to all. I ask my readers to bear in mind that I am not trying to give an exposition of the Dharma. I do hope, however, that I have conveyed something of its distinct taste—the taste of Freedom.

... the teaching is simple.
Do what is right.
Be pure.
At the end of the way is freedom.
Till then, patience.

one

Religious Beginnings

My religious background was, if anything, Quaker. My grandparents would arrive on a Sunday morning in their little white bull—a lumbering cream-coloured Rover, named after Tommy Steele's popular song—and take one, two, or three of us children off with them to the Meeting House. My mother never came. She said she was religious in her own way.

As I jumped down the broad steps under the wooden archway and skipped along the brick path, the old Friends, dressed in their Sunday best, would greet each other, stopping occasionally to ask after my grandmother's hip or to convey an item of news. The atmosphere was friendly and adult. We entered the porch, and made our way through the bustle of the crowded hallway and into the silence of the Meeting Room. We had our own corner and had to walk half-way around the room to reach it. Our shoes clip-clopped on the tiled floor and I wished I didn't feel so self-conscious.

My grandmother brought her own cushions, because of her hip, and my grandfather helped her to get comfortable. I swung my legs quietly and wondered what to think about. I counted the panes of glass in the leaded windows and then I thought that perhaps I ought to say thank you for things.

After fifteen minutes of trying to keep quiet and still, all the children left the room to attend other activities specially designed for them. In the Junior class we were watched over by a pale pastel-coloured poster of a shining 'Gentle Jesus, meek and mild...' or was it the children around him who were meek and mild? And who was it that suffered? They all looked rather too good and adoring for my liking. When we graduated to upstairs we were told stories of Quaker missionaries, and we painted and made models. But the best part was an expedition to the toilet. We always went in twos because we were —or at least I was—just a little bit frightened. We would creep stealthily down the grand, creaking, wooden staircase, trying not to make a sound as all around was so quiet and still, then down a shadowy, narrow corridor until we reached our destination—a large, airy, wood-panelled room which had been incongruously converted into toilets.

Once, when my Quaker days were nearly over, a girl I knew, who had started coming to Meeting of her own accord, stood up and said, 'Do I believe in God?' I was amazed at her courage, not so much because she said what she did —for it was obvious there was no old man up there in the sky—but because she was moved to stand up, in a room full of adults, to communicate her thinking, her doubting. I was struck that she should be thinking so seriously. It had seemed natural to me to wonder about life in the privacy of one's own mind, but now I felt challenged to question openly and to consider the possibility of seeking a deeper understanding.

In the sixth form at school I had to attend lessons in comparative religion given by the headmaster. I didn't like the man and I did my best not to pay attention to him. But when he spoke of Confucius and the Buddha I couldn't help myself. He had unwittingly, good Christian that he was, aroused a serious interest in me, and I was grateful. I borrowed a book from the library which explained how to 'get rid of your ego'. I found the instructions rather disturbing and, not wanting to get rid of anything, I decided that if this was Buddhism I wasn't interested after all. Some years later, when browsing in a bookshop, I came across a slim paperback, a more attractive-looking book about Buddhism by Christmas Humphreys—but to this day I haven't read it. I believe it was the name of the author that really took my fancy: I imagined a very festive, colourful man, outspoken and tending to childlike moods.

Marriage and Meditation

When I was eighteen, I met Ray at the local pub, the 'Bull and Bush'. I was his brother's girlfriend. Gordon was disappearing off the scene, and sometimes when he didn't turn up at the pub, Ray and I would go on to parties without him.

One night, as the party had been near my house, I invited Ray to stay. We were such good friends that it was all quite straightforward. I showed him his room and we sat on the floor drinking tea. We talked about this and that, and then suddenly he was asking me to marry him. He took me in his arms and kissed me. The ground beneath me gave way. I was stunned, flattered, and suddenly in love.

Surely I couldn't say yes just like that—but no reason to say no came to mind. When still at school, only a few months ago, I had decided that I wouldn't get married, but then no one had asked me. I had never dreamt of a proposal like this. It was deadly serious. A flood of thoughts sped around my mind. Would I be sacrificing my planned teaching career? Without understanding why, I knew that I would be. Did I want to spend the rest of my life with this man? Somehow I knew that I would, that my future was already inextricably bound up with him. Wherever it was to take me, I knew what my answer would be—but I waited until morning to give it.

On the morning of our wedding my brother took Ray out for a drink. His purpose, he told me on returning, was to dissuade Ray from marrying me, but Ray, it seemed, would not be moved.

Having failed in his attempt to save Ray, my brother turned his mind to converting the pair of us. He had recently returned from India, and his Christmas present to us was a book on Hatha Yoga. We were ready for the bait. We began to chew our meat in the manner prescribed in the book, and in no time at all we became vegetarians. My brother suggested we join him in attending a yoga class. We took to it enthusiastically, never missing a class and practising religiously at home. Next it was suggested that meditation would follow on quite naturally, and it did. We went along to Pundarika, the London centre of the Friends of the Western Buddhist Order, and after learning to meditate we were keen to find out more about Buddhism.

As we meditated regularly we began to see the possibilities and benefits that lay ahead. We had the potential to deepen our concentration, integrate the bundles of loosely-held-together selves that we were, and develop in our hearts an emotion that was far more profound and all-encompassing than that which we knew of as love.

We learned that negative moods and states of mind need not be put up with, accepted, or excused; we could work to transform them into better, more positive, states. If I felt moody or jealous because I didn't have Ray's attention, I no longer felt justified in blaming him. I had to try to change myself—from within.

We set up a simple shrine. I felt rather self-conscious bowing to it, but I also felt somewhat in awe of the deeply calm and peaceful figure of the Buddha. He seemed to convey with such genuine authority that yes, there was meaning to life after all.

Into our world, which might well have been in danger of narrowing down into a conventional, materialistic one, the perspective of a spiritual life was introduced. Without having made any great effort to pursue the interest aroused in me at school, I had come across a movement which, I instinctively felt, would encourage me to take that interest seriously, to spread my spiritual wings.

In spite of my intuition the night my life merged with Ray's, I went on to train as a teacher. But I found myself struggling to make sense of my training, and I continually questioned what I was doing—and why. As a prospective teacher I was idealistic, although exactly what my ideals amounted to I probably couldn't have said. Before embarking on my training I had had some experience of teaching; now I was frustrated because I couldn't work as I wanted to. Meditation and Buddhism added a steadying influence to my life; they were important to me, but my work and difficulties at college demanded most of my attention. For Ray it was different. He was eager to involve himself in any activities at the Buddhist Centre and he quickly made friends with others in the movement. He had been attending a series of lectures on Tibetan Buddhism given by Sangharakshita, the founder of the FWBO, and he took me along to one. I knew little about Buddhism at that time and this talk, with its fantastic images of wild and wonderful beings, went way over my head. Unlike the attempt to get rid of my ego, it didn't, however, put me off. I liked the friendly atmosphere at the Centre, and I was affected by the appreciation with which the speaker was regarded. I too was impressed by him, despite my inability to follow all he said. It struck me that he really knew what he was talking about, and I was left with a sense that he was quite a remarkable man.

Whilst still at school a friend of mine had announced that although she was intending to marry she wouldn't have any children of her own—there were already too many in the world needing adoption. 'Why even get married?' I had wondered, and I determined not to do so myself.

My determination having given way, I had now been married for a couple of years, and I seemed to be wondering, 'What next?' There was nothing wrong with our marriage, nothing obviously lacking; I just felt a sense of there being further to go in it. When Ray asked me to marry him I didn't consciously think about having children. But the assumption was there. I didn't need to make it conscious—it was the natural outcome of marriage. I began to feel unhappy with what the contraceptive pill might be doing to me, and to see it as a continual reminder that I was deliberately preventing myself from getting pregnant. I was frustrated and unhappy at college. My struggles with my intended career were disturbing me more and more. A friend of mine, Vida, was very pregnant. The idea took hold of me. If I had my own children I could bring them up as I wanted to. I could leave the classroom and start my own. I wanted to be pregnant; I wanted a baby.

Ray, who had been the one keen to get married, was quite happy for us to start a family, although he didn't appear to see it in terms of a fulfilment in the way that I did. For all my naïve ideals and determination, I was a young, happily-married woman, and what was most important to me then was that I should conceive and give birth to my own baby.

I would have given up college there and then, but my mother and my husband persuaded me to see the last few months through and obtain my Teacher's Certificate. I kept up my yoga practice and I tried to meditate, although I found that as my stomach swelled my attention would always wander around the developments within my body.

Despite the preoccupation with my growing stomach, when my exams were over I went along more frequently to the Buddhist Centre. I attended a day retreat there and took part in some exercises designed to improve one's ability to communicate. I was shy by nature and even more introverted in my pregnant state. But I sat through them (I was too shy to do anything else), rather startled to find myself looking so attentively at my brother, my first partner in the exercise, and then embarrassed to be so seemingly intimate with my next, a complete stranger. I was shaken, but none the less inspired, to sample communication in which superficiality was to some extent dispensed with. I began to think more deeply about how I related to others. What was I communicating of myself? And how much did I appreciate, care for, or even see, of others?

Vague glimmerings of an Ideal to be aspired to were stirring in me, albeit largely overshadowed by the insistent presence of my yet unborn baby.

Setting Up Home

With a baby on the way we began to think more seriously about setting up a home and where that might be. We wanted to live in the country. I didn't want to start a family in London. It was the time when old stone cottages in Wales were still cheap, and young couples like ourselves were leaving London to be wet and self-sufficient. We considered doing likewise. We had been involved with the Friends of the Western Buddhist Order for less than a year, but it was now an established part of our lives; so a consideration for us was to be with-in reach of other 'Friends', and we knew of several who were living in Wales. Norfolk was another possibility. We had heard there were some Buddhists trying to develop a community in a godforsaken vil-lage somewhere between Swaffham and the North Sea. The green hills of Wales were more romantic to my mind than the barren and flat realm of East Anglia. But in the end we had neither to search nor to make a choice. A house fell into our laps and it was *en route* to Norfolk. My father offered to rent us one of his cottages in Cambridge.

When my parents separated, my mother and we three children moved to London whilst my father remained in Cambridge. He bought three small, terraced cottages. As, one by one, the sitting ten-ants died, he established his own father in one and himself in another several doors away. When the third cottage, next door to his own, became vacant, he doubled his living space by knocking through the dividing wall upstairs and down. It was this house, from which he had long since moved, that we were offered.

I took great delight in settling into and arranging our new home. The first job to be done was to get rid of the fleas. The carpets were crawling with them. How the previous occupants survived I do not know. They must have had cats for the fleas to live on; now, with no animal in sight, they went for me. I didn't like the idea of killing the fleas; I was, after all, trying not to harm other living beings. However, I couldn't leave them to feed off my new-born baby—and anyway my own legs couldn't take any more.

Then there was the damp and the mould. The cottages were very old. No damp-proof course. Low ceilings. Lots of condensation. Some of the walls had to be painted with anti-fungal, waterproof paint. I particularly enjoyed getting into the walk-in cupboards, one on either side of the fireplace. I had to empty everything out and scrape off whatever I could of the old, flaking paint. Then, when the fresh paint was dry and clean paper covered the shelves, I unpacked all our things. I had the luxury of a whole cupboard in which I could store all my bits and pieces from college days. After living at my mother's and then sharing a flat with a friend, we now had a home of our own to spread into.

The baby's room needed painting. We decided on cornflower blue and white. It was the smallest room and right next to our own bed-room. Our room, at the front, had been, when I was small, my father's. It was the most charming room in the house, with a small, low window overlooking a children's playground, a raised alcove adjoining the sturdy chimney breast, and an alarmingly uneven floor.

It was hard to believe it was safe to walk on. When as children my brother, sister, and I visited my father, we used to crash around like wild things. We never imagined the house would feel the strain. We used to jump on the bed. I even remember my father chasing us across it. Since then the beam that supported the bedroom floor had been reinforced. One could look up at the ceiling from the sitting-room below to see a great crack in the beam, secured by a metal strap. It served to remind us that although the floor was safe, it wasn't sound.

From our bedroom a tiny landing led through to the room at the back of the adjoining cottage. Similarly, a passage had been opened up at the front of the house, downstairs, between the two sitting-rooms. It was a good house in which to play hide-and-seek, although sometimes, as children, we had to beware of the gruff old man hidden beneath a pile of books and papers. He would get us working cata-loguing his files or moving piles of bricks out the back where the old cottages had been knocked down; and then we'd spend our earnings on penny toffee bars from the smelly old shop at the corner.

And now my husband was ensconced in what used to be my father's study. The room was one in which I never felt entirely com-fortable. I would knock a little nervously at the door. I shouldn't really be there. Was I disturbing him?

A Warm Experience

Tittleshall was a couple of hours' drive away from Cambridge. In that quiet, out-of-the-way village, a dilapidated old rectory still just about standing was the home of Sulocana—a reputedly eccentric member of the Western Buddhist Order—her mother, and various sons. Sulocana had once seen the place in a dream, surrounded by Buddhist stupas, and she wanted to turn the dream into reality by establishing a Buddhist community there. For the present she made the house avail-able for retreats. Ray and I were on our way to a weekend retreat at this quaint-sounding place.

We were welcomed into the dimly-lit and dusty hallway and ush-ered up a wide, elegant, visibly decaying staircase and down an uninvitingly dark corridor. We were led, along with several other young people, who I gradually worked out were members or friends of the family rather than retreatants like ourselves, into Granny's apartment. It was a small room in relation to the size of the house, and a complete contrast in terms of atmosphere and comfort. It, too, was dimly lit, but it was warm and cosy, full of furniture, rugs, crocheted shawls, and knick-knacks—and the stream of visitors settled into the armchairs and spaces on the floor. A fire burned, a television flickered, and a kettle whistled. We were offered tea but, before we had a chance to accept, an expectant silence fell around us. Something was about to happen. Having no television of our own, Ray and I had no idea that we had arrived just in time to watch the programme of the week—the adventures of a Buddhist cowboy.

We had soup for supper, sitting on benches around the old rectory table in the cold, cavernous kitchen. The Aga made an attempt to throw out some heat but you had to be pretty close to it to feel it. An old man hovered in the doorway, asking questions about how we had arrived and where we had come from. He turned out to be Tom, a simple-minded old chap from the village who had made the Rectory his second home. I was beginning to work out who was who when several more retreatants arrived. There had as yet been no formal introduction to the retreat. However, I was fading fast and, unable to take in anything more, I decided to escape and retire to bed.

Ray helped me with my bag and showed me where I was to sleep. Bedrooms, on retreats, were always single-sex, but on this occasion we were asked whether we wanted a room together—my heavily pregnant state presumably suggested this special concession. But no, although I was here with my husband, I wanted to participate as fully as I could in every aspect of the retreat. The room was lined with mattresses. As the first woman to arrive, the choice was mine. I took one of the only two beds, situated in the far corner where I would be a little out of the way of the others. I climbed into it and lay there, a little scared and quite bewildered as to what I was involving myself in. Eventually I heard footsteps, whispering, and bags dropping to the floor. I was relieved to find myself no longer alone, but, too shy for introductions, I pretended to be asleep.

In the early morning we meditated in what once would have been a fine drawing-room, facing a many-tiered shrine above which one could gaze out through the French windows on to the wild garden. But concentration was not easy and I suffered from indigestion. We sat on the floor in the same room to do communication exercises, to listen to a tape of one of Sangharakshita's lectures, and to eat soup and talk, or listen to snippets of other people's conversations.

A man called Steve by some, Padmaraja by others, seemed to be in charge. He talked with me and helped me to feel more at ease in this strange environment. I was touched by his warmth and attention. His kind words on parting reduced the discomfort I had experienced to insignificance, and I was left with a positive memory of my first retreat.

I Was a Buddhist

I wanted to give birth to my baby at home. I wanted to do it naturally. I felt quite confident that I could. When I announced my intention to my doctor he tried to persuade me otherwise. He said it was not advisable for a first baby to be born at home, and he told me stories of ambulances and blood running through the night. I wasn't deterred. I knew that the main consideration as far as the doctor was concerned was convenience. I had even heard that babies were sometimes induced in hospital so that they would arrive at a reasonable hour. I asked for a doctor who would agree to my request. The only conditions he laid down were that my midwife must be happy for me to have a home delivery, and that I must be proved to be in good health by having a thorough check-up at the hospital.

On arriving at the hospital I was given a form to fill in. I was astonished at some of the irrelevant questions until I realized that it was assumed that, like the majority of pregnant women, I would deliver in hospital. I asked whether I really needed to fill it all in. Why should I state my religion? I wasn't sure that I had one. And then it dawned on me that it was in case I should die whilst in hospital. Well, I had no intention of doing that. But it did make me think. 'Were your parents Christian? Put that then,' the nurse kindly suggested. 'But I'm not a Christian,' I thought, as I imagined a silver-haired, softly-spoken, clean, dog-collared gentleman praying for me. His prayers would have been wasted. It was at that moment that I realized—I do have a religion; I am a Buddhist. Suddenly my spirits lifted and I was no longer frustrated at being regarded as little more than a statistic. I happily subjected myself to a very superficial 'thorough check-up'. I had been prepared for a waste of time in order that my baby might be born at home. But I left the hospital with more than I'd bargained for. I had made a definite and most meaningful statement about myself.

If the traveler can find
A virtuous and wise companion
Let him go with him joyfully
And overcome the dangers of the way.

two

Out of Place

Whilst my father was away on holiday, his house in Cambridge was used for a men's retreat. My brother was on the retreat and at the end of it he invited Ray and me to join him and a few others for a meal.

I sat at the familiar table, in the house that had never been my own home but which had once belonged to close family friends. A radiant young man appeared from the garden. This was the life, oh! this was the life, he seemed to be saying. Ray was drawn into the lingering retreat atmosphere. He connected, whilst I felt withdrawn, strangely out of place amidst young men heading towards the angelic life, old memories of a large and happy family, and a new life stirring within me.

Later my brother tried to reassure me. He thought I was worried that Ray might want to leave me. I shed a few tears, but my distress was not so specific. It was just hard sometimes feeling I had, almost in one leap, stepped into two conflicting worlds—one foot firmly planted in mundane life and the other drawn towards freedom. Whatever the future was to bring it wasn't a conventional life.

A Baby Arrives

We were still keen yoga practitioners and I was doing shoulder stands until shortly before I was due to give birth.

My contractions began in the evening. They were fairly strong and regular so we telephoned the midwife. She came and felt my swollen stomach, decided that I was on my way but that it was a slow start. I should go off to bed and call her if the contractions came more frequently or increased in strength. I didn't sleep very well that night—not so much from discomfort as from anxious anticipation. I was surprised and a bit disappointed to find that nothing much was happening when I woke up. However, before I had really decided to get up, occasional waves of tightening started up again. Thank goodness, I really was going into labour. Whilst I waited for the midwife I checked my list of requirements. A table by my bed held a collection of rather strange items, all waiting patiently for this moment. I still needed some newspapers—I didn't know why—but Ray would get those. I made up the little white canvas cot that I had once been small enough to fit into, and then, exhausted, got back into bed. I wanted to remain as active as I could; with all the yoga I'd been doing I thought I wouldn't have much trouble, and really I wanted to give birth squatting. That, apparently, was the most natural way. But the contractions went on and on relentlessly, getting nowhere, it seemed, except to wear me out. The midwife wanted to give me an injection of pethidine, even though I had warned her beforehand that I didn't want to take anything of the sort. She told me I had a long way to go yet; it would serve to give me some rest, and it would definitely have worn off before I needed to start pushing. Ray was anxious for me to have it too. I gave in and succumbed to the relief it offered me. But I didn't like the woozy effect on my mind. My awareness was dulled and confused, and I so wanted to be alert for the birth of my child. The midwife would have doped me up again but she saw how determined I was and instead she struck a bargain with me. If I drank up all my rose-hip syrup (I needed the energy), she wouldn't give me another injection. I sipped away, and more or less finished it.

I really had thought it would be easier than it was. There was no way I could get myself up into a squatting position. I simply tried to do what I was told. I got muddled up with my breathing and pushing —oh, why hadn't I practised more?

At long, long last the painful business was over. I stretched out my arms to hold my baby as soon as the midwife had made her cry. But the cord must be cut first; then she was wrapped in one of the prepared pieces of old sheeting, and handed to me.

The doctor arrived too late for the birth, although it seemed that his presence was merely a formality to ensure that the midwife carried out her job satisfactorily. And then my mother arrived to see her first grandchild taking a bath. I noticed that since the birth Ray had spent much of his time downstairs. I discovered later that he had been extremely worried. With so much activity going on in the bedroom and with people coming in and out—especially the big, heavy-footed doctor—he was worried that the floor might finally give way. He had been standing in the room below, looking up to see if further signs of strain were showing on the strapped-up beam.

I kept the baby beside me, snug and warm in her white canvas cot. I lay awake listening to every sound she made. She began to hiccup, and with great concern I took her in my arms to soothe her.

Soon after her arrival we moved out of our bedroom—Ray was too worried about the floor giving way—and into the large one at the back of the house. I didn't agree with the midwife that we should keep the room constantly heated throughout the night. However, I did begin to dread getting up in the night to feed the baby, and I would have given anything for central heating or a gas fire. I would immediately switch the convector heater on but still I shivered as I changed the nappy, sometimes the sheets too, and sat up to feed.

The duties of motherhood kept me busy and mostly quite happy. I was constantly aware of my baby, ready to respond to all her needs. I loved holding her, feeding her, watching her kick her little legs and gurgle with delight. In a very basic way I was satisfied. But I couldn't talk to my baby. I too needed someone to respond to my needs for human warmth and communication. I would then appear at Ray's office door, offering him a cup of coffee and hoping for some attention.

It was a cold November when the baby was born, and I was in no hurry to venture out with her. Then one sunny afternoon I decided it was time for my baby to see the outside world, and for me to re-establish myself in it. I put her into the pram for the very first time and took her off, so bravely, down the hill and into the college grounds. I had no real purpose there; just to be out with my pram and its treasured contents, getting a little exercise and taking in the fresh air. I found that out of the confines of my own home I began to feel rather small, insignificant, and lonely. For nine months I had been special, with this baby growing inside me. We made up a little world together and I prepared a comfortable, secure home for her to be born into. When I went into labour I was the centre of the universe. And when my baby was born I was such a proud and contented mother. The world had been revolving around me. But now, outside, wandering aimlessly along pathways and across lawns, sitting on a bench to watch the world go by, I was noticed by no one. I was simply another young mother out with her baby. I almost felt as though I had been fooled. Had someone pulled the wool over my eyes? Had I tricked myself? The world I had brought my daughter into wasn't so warm, safe, and intimate after all. And she was already separate from me. I had brought her into a world apart from me—a vast, unfriendly world, a world of suffering. She slept peacefully, unaware of my feelings of loneliness and my unsettling thoughts.

A House Full of Women

Within the FWBO, single-sex activities had begun to gather momentum. That winter (1973) separate retreats were planned for men and women. Bhante was going to be leading a seminar for men at the old rectory in Norfolk, and Ray had booked to go. Dhammadinna and Marichi, two of the very few women Order members, were looking for a suitable venue for a women's retreat. I don't remember how the suggestion first came about, but my house in Cambridge was considered a possibility. It wasn't in the countryside, but the college grounds were close by. If it wasn't to be a large retreat we could fit everyone in, and even if we were a little squashed, it would mean we would keep warm. But the main point for me was that if the retreat were to be held in my house, I could, along with my three-month-old baby, take part in it.

There were about eight of us on the retreat. Ray's office was turned into a dormitory with mattresses on the floor. We even managed to accommodate a woman who was confined to a wheelchair. Suddenly my house was full of women, most of whom I had never met before. I allowed them to take over my kitchen and rearrange my sitting-room, maintaining a degree of control because I knew where everything was or should have been; only I knew how to light and tend the old ceramic stove. And I had my baby to look after, so if I wanted to I could always retreat into another world with her.

The woman in the wheelchair had to be very careful with her diet. She could only digest skimmed milk. Someone else had to eat seaweed. Around the kitchen table there was a lot of talk about diet—how certain foods were bad for you and others were rich in this and that. I was fascinated. My grandmother used to call white sugar the 'bowl of death', but I hadn't realized there were so many nasty substances one had to watch out for—if, that is, one had a mind to. They talked together quite freely, openly and at great length, about themselves and in particular, or so it seemed, about diet and bodily ailments. I was the only mother and as such I could have assumed an air of authority. Occasionally I was referred to. I would have liked to hold their attention for a little longer but I didn't know how. It was enough trying to keep up with them, let alone break through my shyness and talk more myself.

My baby still slept for a good part of the day and so I was able to attend most of the retreat programme. Sometimes I would bring her into the shrine-room for the early morning meditation and sit her in her 'bouncy chair'. She was usually very quiet and contented; occasionally she would utter gentle murmurings. I couldn't really meditate but I could participate in the atmosphere of the room and I felt much happier and less alone than if I had been hanging around out of the way upstairs.

I had a baby alarm fitted up so that from the shrine-room I could hear when my daughter had woken up. I would sit beneath it, by the door to the stairs, so that if necessary I could quietly disappear in order to attend to her. Sometimes when I experienced a lot of resistance to meditation I would be relieved by a little cry coming through on the loudspeaker. I would then be glad to slip quietly out of the shrine-room and happily attend to my baby's needs. Occasionally someone might offer to mind her for me but I didn't really want them to.

Sometimes at night I felt particularly miserable and alone. I had to drag myself out of bed to feed a hungry baby. I would then keep her in bed with me for comfort—as though this tiny little bundle could offer me some protection.

We managed to gather up enough chairs and arrange them in intimate pairs for communication exercises. I had only just put my daughter down to sleep so I had no reason to excuse myself. I was relieved to find I wasn't the only one who had considered escape. I felt very shy when Dhammadinna sat down in front of me but as the exercises went on I experienced an extraordinarily powerful flow of warmth in our communication.

We listened to one of Sangharakshita's lectures entitled 'Breaking through to Buddhahood'. I was deeply moved by his description of how, by putting ourselves into new situations, we could loosen up, even change, our own firmly rooted conditioning. From that time on I was inspired by the figure of Vajrapani (the wrathful Bodhisattva of energy) and the idea of breaking through from the mundane to the transcendental.

When the retreat came to an end I was both relieved to have my home to myself again and sorry to be saying goodbye to my new friends. It had been, on the whole, a worthwhile, though rather uncomfortable, experience. Enough, however, was enough.

Ray arrived home from his retreat, full of it. He had had a wonderful time exploring the rambling old rectory with its maze of storerooms and outhouses, one of which Sulocana had turned into a pottery.

On his retreat it seemed there had been a lot of talk about community living. And it wasn't simply for the benefit of single men. Ray, too, was inspired and he told me of an idea of having two communities in the country, at a little distance from each other: men in one, women in the other; young children with their mothers, boys at a certain age joining their fathers. They had obviously discussed the issue of interaction between the two communities and Ray's account was that they thought it would probably work most harmoniously if women didn't enter the men's domain but that men, or some of them—the fathers at least—could visit the women's community.

I listened to his enthusiastic talk. I wasn't really ready to hear it. I could have done with a little time settling cosily back into our home together. But we had gone too far. I gathered up the dirty washing and, standing over the soapy steam of the machine I'd chosen with such housewifely care, I knew that I couldn't argue. In the light of our spiritual aspirations it made sense to consider living separately in single-sex communities. I even felt a slight attraction to the idea. An uncomfortable feeling inside me told me that one day we would do it. One day, but not, oh not, just yet.

Too Shy to Ask

When we were still living in London Ray became a Mitra. Mitra is the Sanskrit word for friend. In a simple ceremony he demonstrated his intention to follow the Buddhist path under the guidance of Sangharakshita, and to deepen his association with others following that path. In the course of the ceremony, two Order members became his special friends, his Kalyana Mitras who, themselves committed Buddhists, would be particularly concerned with his spiritual welfare. In becoming a Mitra he had established a formal connection with the FWBO. I knew that my own involvement in the movement was serious, but I didn't then appreciate the point of making such a declaration myself.

My brother was now ordained as a member of the Order and he had become Lokamitra—a friend of the world. He and his girlfriend, Dhammadinna, had come up from London to visit us; *en route*, I believe, for Norfolk, where Bhante (as Sangharakshita was known within the movement) was then living. Dhammadinna took the opportunity of an evening alone with me to draw me out. She gently encouraged me to see for myself that what I wanted was, naturally, to become a Mitra. The important question was 'Who should be my Kalyana Mitras?' I didn't know many Order members, or at least none of them very well; having moved away from London, and with a young baby to look after, I was not in a good position to further my acquaintances. Dhammadinna kindly offered herself. She was certainly the Order member I felt most at ease with. Who else did I know? Well, on the weekend retreat I'd attended I had been touched by the friendliness Padmaraja had shown towards me. Dhammadinna knew him well, and she thought that between the three of us we could develop a Kalyana Mitra relationship.

The next step in the procedure was to inform Bhante of the proposal, and ask if he would be happy for the relationship to be formalized.

An opportunity for speaking directly with Bhante was shortly presented to me when he spent a night with us in Cambridge. Dhammadinna was staying too—presumably on her return from Norfolk. In fact we had a house full: John, a lively lad from Scotland, so energetic he could hardly keep still; Mark, so quiet one hardly noticed him; and Lokamitra was there too.

After breakfast we removed to the sitting-room. Ray and I had asked Bhante to give our daughter a name; she was five months old and, not happy with the name I had originally chosen, I had simply been calling her 'baby'. Now Bhante took the yellow-clad baby into his arms and, as she looked up at him with a very serious expression, he announced that he had chosen the name Shanti for her. It meant 'peaceful', and it was, and still remains, a very appropriate name.

So this was my opportunity. I was sitting on a low stool, almost literally at Bhante's feet. All I had to do was to catch his attention and put my request to him. But I couldn't do it. Not because I didn't want to. The asking now meant so much to me that I was overcome with shyness, and I simply couldn't summon up the courage to speak. Eventually Bhante rose to go. I still hadn't spoken, and so it was to my great relief that Dhammadinna stepped in, just as he was leaving, and put the question for me. I felt embarrassed and frustrated by my shyness and my inability to speak for myself. However, the incident served to heighten my awareness that I wasn't entering into this relationship lightly and that to become a Mitra meant a great deal to me.

The ceremony took place in Bhante's home at Castle Acre. Bhante, sitting cross-legged on the floor by the side of a shrine, warmly waved the three of us in to take our places opposite him. I sat between Dhammadinna and Padmaraja, and we committed ourselves to friendship in the context of the spiritual life. It was like a marriage, said Bhante, in that we were bound to each other. But our bonds were not those of romantic attachment, and we would love one another not simply 'for better or for worse' but for 'the Good'—that is, we would always look for and encourage the best in one another as we made our way towards Enlightenment. The implication that a spiritual bond was of far greater significance than the conventional one of marriage gave me much food for thought.

Mitrata

Mitrata was the FWBO's bimonthly publication designed for Mitras. Padmaraja, my Kalyana Mitra, was the editor. I remember receiving my first copy from him: it was almost like opening a love-letter, so much did both it and the 'warmest regards' of the sender mean to me. With Shanti asleep and Ray working in his office, I read the magazine from cover to cover: the editorial depicting the true friend, an extract from one of Bhante's lectures, and questions and answers from one of his seminars on a Buddhist text.

As a Mitra I could now meet with other Mitras and Order members to study the Dharma, the teaching of the Buddha. In practice this was very difficult as the groups were held in London. But Ray frequently had to go to London on business so sometimes I would accompany him and, leaving Shanti with my mother, go along to a study group. We met in the three-storeyed house where David was squatting. His room was at the very top of the stairs, behind a curtain, gloomily candle-lit and strewn with dark cloths and bedspreads. I remembered David from yoga classes. There was a girl with long, bright orange hair, and Colin, an artist who had hair just as long at the back but startlingly short on top. The book we were studying was a hefty one —Bhante's *A Survey of Buddhism*—and progress was slow as we examined and discussed each sentence. I was quite happy to read when it came to my turn, but otherwise I hardly uttered a word.

As time went on I was sometimes able to take part in an Order-Mitra day. These were occasions when Order members and Mitras came together to meditate, study, listen to a talk, and get to know one another better. They provided an opportunity in which to practise the Dharma more intensively than one's normal circumstances might allow. On one of these I overheard another Mitra relating his problem with mental chatter, the voice in one's head that just went rabbiting on and on, leaving one with no inner peace. I was surprised to find someone else describing my problem, but unfortunately I heard no simple solution. Having embarked on the path to perfection I was hoping for quick results. But listening to the Dharma, it seemed, was one thing; understanding it and putting it into practice was another.

There seemed to be only one other young mother seriously involved in the movement. My Kalyana Mitras encouraged me to meet up with her and so, whenever I went to London, I took Shanti in her carry-cot to the flat where Jinamata lived with her daughter, Lila. The girls were too young to be able to play together; nevertheless it was a relief just to drink tea with another Buddhist who was also a mother, even though we were so different. She had her life highly organized, and would be working on her doctoral thesis half-way through the night, and at any spare moment she had during the day.

I had wanted and hoped for more. I was still in contact with my friend Vida, from whom I had 'caught' pregnancy. She and her family had also moved out of London, a little nearer to Norfolk than we had managed. But our communication was limited: by her husband, television, dope, cooking, and children. Occasionally it would go a little deeper, if we went for a walk without the men, or even when shopping at the local supermarket. We had known one another for two years, and there was more genuine friendship between us than I could expect to establish with Jinamata over an occasional cup of tea. I couldn't, however, share with her the tender shoots of spiritual enquiry that were seeking nourishment within me.

Learning to Drive

For my seventeenth birthday I was given a course of ten driving lessons. I didn't get on very well, had little practice outside the lessons, and by the time the course came to an end I had no money to continue.

When I was twenty-three Ray and I owned a car, a green Mini-Traveller which we had bought from my mother. Once I had lost my stomach and could leave my new-born baby for an hour or so, I set out again to learn to drive. We were, after all, working to become less dependent on one another and to be more individual. I needed and wanted the sort of independence that being able to drive would give me.

My driving instructor was a funny little man. I didn't like him at first and wondered whether I should try someone else. He was a bit unfriendly and sharp with me. But after several lessons I began to find I was looking forward to them. What I was looking forward to, I eventually admitted to myself—though feeling rather confused about it—was being in my instructor's company and the attention that he gave me. A definite attraction had arisen between us.

A little harmless flirting went on, but nothing out of the ordinary— until, on the day of my test, as I announced triumphantly to him that I'd passed, he overstepped the mark, took me in his arms and kissed me. I was thrilled to have passed, and then excited even more by his embrace. Back at the office he told me of the course on motorway driving that was recommended for new drivers. In my slightly intoxicated state I almost signed up—I wouldn't then have to say goodbye to him. But no, I had done what I had set out to do, I couldn't linger any more. I walked home, my excitement slightly dampened and disturbed by the inappropriate tugging at my heart.

Some weeks later, whilst out shopping, I caught sight of the car I had learnt to drive in, and there he was in the passenger seat. He saw me and waved. His eyes sparkled with a look of warm recognition and I watched, my heart beating wildly, as he disappeared out of sight. The traffic lights changed and I forced myself to push the pram across the road and continue on my way to Sainsburys. For several weeks I found myself keenly watching out, wondering and hoping, whenever I went into the city. Whilst trying to become more individual I was quietly pining for attention. And learning to drive, it appeared, wasn't necessarily going to make me independent.

*Like garlands woven from a
heap of flowers,
Fashion from your life as
many good deeds.*

three

A Golden Ray

In August 1974 Ray, Shanti, and I were on retreat together at a country house called Four Winds. Ray was to be ordained.

My shoulders ached from sitting in meditation. I stood alone looking out over the garden, hoping no one would approach me. But I was glad when Mangala did, and we had a gentle, easy conversation.

We sat on the floor for our meals and I spoon-fed Shanti whilst we ate. As the ordinations drew near we spent more and more time in silence. When our meals were to be eaten in silence, Lokamitra thought it was too distracting to have a baby in our midst. With Dhammadinna to help soften the blow, he had a quiet word with me. Of course I felt rejected. I took Shanti down to the bottom of the garden and we sat together behind a hedge to eat our lunch.

Ray had been sharing a room with me, but when someone left the retreat he moved into the empty room to be more alone in preparation for his ordination.

On the night of the private ordinations I took Shanti along to the shrine-room, hoping she might fall asleep. But she was too lively. As I walked through the house, returning to my room, I met Bhante on his way to conduct the ceremony. I was so sorry I would have to miss the evening.

The next day, however, both Shanti and I were able to attend the public ordination ceremony. It was an extremely happy and colourful occasion. I felt slightly bewildered though when my husband was no longer recognizable: in the course of the ceremony he had been given a new name—Sona. And then I saw that Ray had turned to gold.*

* The Pali word *sona* means gold.

Moving On

We had decided to look for a house in Norfolk. Cambridge was, after all, simply a stepping-stone. Now, with the addition of a baby into our life we felt the need to live within easy reach of other Buddhists more acutely . We had established a nuclear family. If we were serious about moving away from an identification with the 'group' and towards individuality, we had to ease our dependence on our own particular unit and develop a less isolated, more expansive way of living.

We began to look around, with the old rectory as our focal point. There were now two men living there with the family: John, and an Order member, Ratnapani. Devamitra, another Order member, was about to move up that way. Mike, from Cornwall, who was shortly to be ordained, visited us in Cambridge, and he too considered moving with his family to Norfolk.

We drove around the North Norfolk towns, visiting estate agents and one or two properties. We stayed the night at the old rectory and Ratnapani gave us the use of his room. Shanti was ready for bed so I took her upstairs. Ratnapani was still in his room, in conversation with Bhante, but he ushered me in nevertheless. I set up the little white cot, changed Shanti's nappy, and settled her down to sleep, all the while feeling like an intruder and highly conscious of the fact that Bhante, the Venerable Sangharakshita, was walking up and down, talking very intensely with Ratnapani, completely undistracted by my presence.

Every time a letter arrived with details of a house for sale we would wonder excitedly whether this was the one. But even if it looked ideal on paper there was always something not quite right when we came to view the actual property. I began to get rather despondent. Walking back home from the city centre, having done my shopping, I would plod up the hill hoping, almost expecting, to find that something had happened that would change my life. I had a nice home, as good a husband as I could have wished for, and a delightful baby. But I was unsettled. Something was missing and I had a feeling it was beyond me to find it. At least, I thought, if we could find a house in or near Tittleshall....

A couple from London, both Mitras, were interested in living in closer association with other Buddhist families. Sulocana wanted more Buddhists to move into the old rectory. The suggestion was eventually voiced. What if Sona and I, and Ray and Jaya from London, together with our children, moved in?

At last we had a definite proposition, which would help us to move on from nuclear family life, to consider. Sona was keen. I took my time to come round and then, although nervous, I was inspired by the positive challenge. Although I liked having my own home, my sense of there being more to life than that, and of the need to push myself a bit—away from the clutches of habitual, conditioned behaviour—got the better of me.

But Ray and Jaya were not after all ready for such a move. However, Mike, now ordained as Abhaya, was interested in living in the old rectory whilst he continued to look for a house for his family. Why didn't we move in and take things from there?

Abhirati

In the autumn of 1974 the old rectory became our new home and, to mark the attempt to transform it into a Buddhist community, it was renamed Abhirati—the abode of intense delight. Overlooking the lawn at the side of the house were two large, well-proportioned, virtually identical rooms, with what was once perhaps a corridor but now a decent-sized, though rather plain, room in between them. Sona and I chose the room to the right at the top of the stairs. The other one, which had a little dressing-room leading off it, might have been more convenient, but it didn't get quite as much sun, and was, in an unspecific way, less attractive.

All our furniture fitted easily into this one room. Even the old ceramic stove, which we had salvaged from Cambridge, was rigged up in the hope that it would warm us more effectively than the open fire could. Once again there were cupboards, not so deep this time, on each side of the fireplace. Clothes went into one and everything else that needed to be put away went into the other.

Shanti was to sleep in the corridor room next to us. It took a little while for her to settle in there. Often I would end up keeping her in bed with us, rather than hanging around in the cold wondering if the house really was haunted.

With a coat of paint, curtains, a rug on the floor, and a few toys scattered about, it became her room. Then Abhaya arrived from Cornwall complete with his wife, Val, and the kids, Danny and Louise. He had persuaded Val to move into Abhirati whilst he continued to look for a house of their own. For the time being we tried to live as a community. We thought the children could share, so Danny and Louise moved in with Shanti. I was a little concerned to hear that Danny had a habit of waking in the night, but I wasn't prepared for the screams he let forth when he did wake. I did my best to muck in and sometimes tried to pacify him when no one else seemed to have heard. But after a while my patience wore thin, and when I woke to both his and Shanti's cries I would curse him. I was annoyed that I had agreed to the children sharing. Now I would have to move Shanti.

Sona had begun to use the little dressing-room as an office. Sulocana's eldest son Caron, the wild Caron, named most unsuitably after a French cosmetic, had been the last inhabitant, and had left it strewn with old animal skins and related objects. Just as one had to beware when looking in the fridge in case Caron had put a freshly run-over owl in it, just so did one tread carefully in this room. Sona cleared it up as best he could and made it look quite grand with a plush red carpet that he'd found stored away somewhere now laid out on the floor. With a fire burning in the grate it became quite a pleasant room for him to work in. But when it was cold and empty it had a strange feel to it and I didn't like going inside. It was in there, however, that Shanti would have to sleep.

It was only a few steps further to her new room, but I had to step out into the main corridor at the top of the stairs to get there. I always had to brace myself and, for Shanti's sake, pretend I wasn't afraid. I would walk her round and round that little room until she fell asleep again. I felt a bit guilty—I wouldn't want to sleep in that room—but what else could I do? It *would* have been very convenient if we had chosen differently from the start.

Shanti was only just beginning to walk when we moved into Abhirati. With the cold stone floors, the dirt and dust, and the dangers of rotting wood and tools left lying expectantly about, it was not the best time to arrive; but then we didn't plan it. I had to watch her every move, and she couldn't often wear her yellow dungarees.

We took turns to cook and to make bread. Sometimes it would all be eaten as soon as it had come out of the oven. There was plenty of goat's milk—a novelty at first until you found almost everything smelling of goats.

I had been looking forward to the arrival of Abhaya's family. The children, I imagined, would play with Shanti and keep her amused, and Val would be company for me. The men sometimes used to get together of an evening at one of the local pubs. I never wanted to join them, and I was glad that Sona had the opportunity to work and play with other men—but still I was envious. Sulocana was not a woman to get close to; she was always preoccupied, living in some other world. I was caught up with a young child, but Val, on whom I'd pinned my hopes, was too domesticated, and her interest in Buddhism was so vague. She was, to my mind, far too easygoing with her children, and we couldn't possibly have discussed or interfered with the bringing-up of one another's offspring.

Whilst Sona moved towards other men I tried not to depend on him so much for intimacy and deeper communication. We both felt the strain, and I found it hard not to feel a bit lonely in my striving. When he decided to have his own single mattress on the floor, wanting more space, I cried silently, wishing for my part that there wasn't so much of it around.

Sometimes I would put Shanti on the back of my bike and cycle across the countryside to visit my old friend, Vida, who had recently bought a house several miles away. I longed for some meaningful communication, the friendship of kindred spirits. Our meetings were always warm and friendly but they seemed to revolve around children and the washing machine, and my particular hunger was never satisfied.

Fion, Sulocana's youngest son, who had just given up school to educate himself at home, was often my most stimulating company. In spite of his contempt for Buddhists he seemed to enjoy living with us all. Sometimes if there was a fire in the library I would sit there rather than alone up in my own room. Fion would tell me a hundred and one things I didn't know until Johnny, one of Jane-from-the-cottage's numerous children, appeared, and they would proceed to tease Danny mercilessly and romp about like five-year-olds. Sulocana would darn socks or stitch away at the shirt that was to be Damion's birthday present. She spun wool and dyed it with natural dyes. I admired the skeins of subtly-coloured wool. In another life, perhaps if we'd gone to Wales, I too would have been spinning and dyeing. But where, apart from producing a beautiful pullover, would it have led? Instead, I was struggling to loosen and disentangle the threads that bound me to this life and, in particular, to my husband.

Sometimes it seemed a crazy thing to be doing, detaching myself from the man I loved, but a deep conviction led me on. Despite appearances to the contrary I knew that I was not going against the intuition I had experienced the night he asked me to marry him. I still felt a connection with Sona that I was convinced would last throughout our lives, perhaps even beyond. But if that connection was to be one of real love, of genuine concern for one another, rather than the reliance of one half upon another, we had to continue our efforts to stand on our own two feet.

Sulocana's fourth son would come home during the holidays. I got rather annoyed with him for being so careless, especially when Shanti fell down the stairs after he had left the gate—rigged up to prevent her climbing—open. I didn't realize that his behaviour was due to anything more than general rebellion against the Buddhists in his house until Sulocana announced, almost accusingly, that the poor boy was attracted to me.

I started smoking roll-ups with Abhaya, desperately wanting attention and some respite from the growing tension. I felt I couldn't turn to Sona.

Whenever I got the opportunity I would sit upstairs and transcribe one of Bhante's lectures on the Noble Eightfold Path. It was a wonderful way to study, and helped me get a perspective on why I had chosen this peculiar habitat. I was reminded that I was not just reading about the Path—I was treading it too. I had had my own experience of the first stage, the stage of Perfect Vision. I had had my own glimpse into the true nature of existence. I knew that marriage and babies, and even a vocational career, were not ultimately going to satisfy me. I wanted to sharpen my vision and transform my life in accordance with it.

John had appointed himself treasurer. He instigated house meetings which were meant to give us an opportunity to discuss the running of the household, ideas for improving our environment, and spiritual projects we wanted to pursue. John would arrive at whichever room we were meeting in, very business-like, with the accounts and a notebook in which to write up any minutes that were required. The misunderstanding, confusion, and polarization that went on between the Buddhists and the family often left us feeling frustrated and upset, and we were usually glad when a meeting was over. We did very well, under the circumstances, trying to live as a Buddhist community, but no matter how much Sulocana dreamt and talked of the place as such, she actually seemed to like it exactly as it was—a sadly decaying, ramshackle old building, home for two to five sons, one granny, and an assortment of fellow Buddhists and their children. It was the Rawnsley home, and although we were given free rein to discuss the potential of the place, to plan, and even to begin to execute improvements, nothing ever got very far. Perhaps the greatest achievement was fitting a shower in one of the storerooms by the kitchen. But it was so cold in there that only the very hardy ever used it. Once Val and I found ourselves in the kitchen, with Sulocana apparently well out of the way. We set to cleaning out the cupboards and tidying up the shelves, nervously listening out in case we should be caught. But what was the point? By tomorrow it would all have returned to normal.

A Little Passion

Sometimes I would join Sona on his business trips to London. I liked staying with him at my mother's house. Away from the tensions of our rambling life at Abhirati we had a chance to be more intimate with one another. On one occasion we were more intimate than I had been prepared for, and after a quick calculation we gave in to the welcome embrace of passion.

I hadn't thought I wanted another child. One was enough to satisfy my maternal instinct, and so long as she had friends to mix with I felt no need to have another. A second child would simply tighten the bonds I was trying to loosen, and restrict me even more. I watched Val, who was quite content to be the mother of two (she probably would have liked more), as she lived her life around her children. I didn't want to be like that.

When I realized that I was probably pregnant I had mixed feelings. There we were, trying to ease ourselves out of our dependence on one another and edging away from living as a family unit, and now it looked as though another baby was on its way to join us. What a nuisance! However, we had been aware that we had taken a risk. After the initial shock of hearing that I definitely was pregnant, and in spite of the setback it could cause in my spiritual career, I couldn't help being pleased.

The prospect of another child was the catalyst for our leaving Abhirati. As I settled into the pregnancy I began to long for a home of our own: a separate nest where I could concentrate on my own offspring without having to be so closely involved with two other families; a kitchen that I could organize as I wanted, of which I would be in charge; and bedrooms within easy reach of each other, so that when a child cried at night I wouldn't have to brace myself to embark on a cold, dark journey through the probably haunted corridors.

If we hadn't succumbed to passion that night we might have stayed at Abhirati a little longer. We might have gone on to share a house with Abhaya and Val. But sooner or later we would have left the old rectory to Sulocana and her sons, gathering dust, Caron's endless clay pots, and dreams.

A Place in the Order

I was pregnant with my second child and still living in the community at Abhirati when—in July 1975—I was ordained into the Western Buddhist Order. My ordination took place on a weekend retreat in the middle of Thetford Forest.

In the course of study led by Bhante, one Order member, married with a family, commented that there seemed to be no place in the Order for someone like him. I was shocked to hear him say such a thing. Shy as I was, I had to object. How could that be true when here I was about to be welcomed into the Order?

When I discussed my ordination request with Bhante, in the light of my being pregnant with my second child, he didn't turn me away. But perhaps that Order member, now resigned, was right. There is no room in the Order for one who considers himself first a member of a family and only secondly a member of the spiritual community. It took me a long while to appreciate the real significance of the fact that 'commitment was primary, life-style secondary'. In theory I believed that commitment to the Buddha, the Dharma, and the Sangha came before commitment to my family. But in practice it didn't always work out like that. I couldn't attend an Order weekend because my children needed looking after. I couldn't give adequate time to my friends because my children were vying for attention. I couldn't move into a women's community. I chose to get married and to start a family, and then I chose not to make marriage and family the be-all and end-all of my existence. I felt limited in my second choice by my first. I had to fulfil the responsibilities I had initially undertaken, but I had to fulfil them within the context of Going for Refuge, not as ends in themselves. I had to accept that I had limited myself, but I also had to appreciate that if I was stuck for a babysitter it didn't necessarily mean that I was lacking in commitment.

Dhammadinna shared my room the night I was ordained. She wondered how I liked my new name—perhaps hoping I might let it slip before it was announced the following day. Padmaraja was sure I would be a lotus—but I wasn't. That night I ceased to be Jane. I declared that my only security, my only Refuge, was to be found in the Buddha, the Dharma, and the Sangha. I became Srimala. It didn't occur to me to consider whether I liked my name or not. When Bhante gave it to me that was simply who I was—Srimala, an auspicious garland of flowers dedicated to the Path to Enlightenment.

There is pleasure
And there is bliss
Forgo the first to possess
the second.

four

Love Shines Through

A few miles out of Tittleshall, on the way to Norwich, we found a semi-detached cottage in the village of Great Ryburgh. There were some awkward things about it but on the whole we were pleased with it. Sona made plans for the work that needed doing. There was water—a single tap in the back porch—but no toilet. If I wanted my baby to be born at home we had to have an inside toilet, a bath, and running hot water. We decided to extend the kitchen and remove the stairs from it. We had a friend who could build us an open-plan staircase (very popular at the time) leading from the front room up to the two bedrooms. A bathroom and small spare room would be built in place of the existing lean-to.

Our neighbours had by far the better deal with the garden. We had a narrow strip in comparison with their extensive grounds. They had lots of flowers, an orchard, a vegetable patch, and a garage. To reach our garden we had to climb up a steep incline. There was scope to put up a washing line, grow a few vegetables, and have something of a lawn. But to begin with we erected a shed to house the chemical toilet.

Sona and friends began work on the cottage whilst we still lived at Abhirati. When the major extension work was more or less complete, we moved in. It was like camping out on a building site, covered in cement and saw-dust. At times it was thoroughly depressing, at others, our plans and our imagination kept us going.

The bathroom and running hot water were ready just in time.

Sona had been reading D.H. Lawrence and he told me that he didn't believe in love. I was in no mood for any philosophical discussion on the matter. I tried not to take it personally. If there was one thing I wanted just then it was love—or at least an obvious display of affection and understanding for my state of body and mind.

He wasn't unpleasant to me but rather, from my point of view, a bit insensitive. I sat in the evenings crocheting, absorbed with the fullness of my stomach, and the concern as to whether I had prepared adequately enough for the imminent event that would, once again, change my life dramatically. He read his book and occasionally commented on Lawrence's views.

Dhammadinna came to stay and so did my mother. It was good to have others around to give Sona and me the attention that we couldn't give each other. We were both in need of it.

On 7 December my contractions began. They were quite gentle but I had a feeling—or was it a hope?—that this was probably it, and so Sona went off to the phone-box to call the midwife. Yes, labour had definitely begun, she said, after looking at me for a while, but she thought it would still be quite some time. We should call her again later when things hotted up. She stayed for a cup of tea, and as we drank, the gentle gripping on my stomach came on more frequently and more intensely. I could no longer concentrate on the conversation going on around me. Perhaps you should go up to your bed, suggested the midwife, not so convinced now that she would be going anywhere. My mother took Shanti out for the afternoon and I took myself upstairs to get into bed in the middle of the day. I hadn't been there long when labour began in earnest, surprising the midwife and convincing her that a baby really was on its way. For a while I wished I hadn't gone to bed. Why couldn't I have tried squatting? But as the contractions continued to gain in strength I was glad to be there, writhing around in agony and then leaning back exhausted on my pillows. Two years previously I had done the same thing. But nothing prepares you. The pain was becoming unbearable. I simply couldn't believe I could stand any more. But there was Sona, holding my hand, and I could see in his eyes how much he cared about me.

A New Life in Brighton?

A few days after the birth of my second daughter I received a congratulatory card, the message on which was Blake's poem 'Infant Joy'. I decided to call my delightful baby Joy, until the time came for Bhante to name her. Bhante's choice was Sundari, which means beautiful. It was another very appropriate choice for not only was she a beautiful baby, she is now a beautiful young woman. How fortunate I was, I reflected, I now had Peace and Beauty in my life.

By the time Sundari was a few months old I was frustrated living in Great Ryburgh. I had been glad that we had bought our own house. It had served its purpose, but it wasn't destined to be a dream family home. Living at Abhirati had been our first step towards extricating ourselves from the conventional mould of the nuclear family. In a sense we had backtracked on our efforts by moving to Great Ryburgh, although I think it was an important move for me—and probably for Sona too—as a basis from which to take a further step. We had found the nearest thing to a dream cottage in the country. I had had a nest into which my second child could be born. I had baked my own bread and made rose-hip syrup. But still my life wasn't complete. Delightful as that existence could be at times, it would take us nowhere but round in circles if we didn't keep making an effort to develop spiritually.

Sona had started up a yoga class in the nearby town of Fakenham. We had ideas of forming a meditation group and building up activities around us. We'd met several people who had moved to Norfolk looking for an alternative way of living. They enjoyed the challenge of an occasional yoga class, but they wanted to carry on smoking dope. They weren't really interested in a radically alternative life-style. One of our 'self-sufficient' neighbours was always trying to find out what we did for pleasure. How did we relax? He seemed to equate our being Buddhists with being on our best behaviour, and he couldn't understand when we said that Buddhism was not merely one interest amongst others but that it affected every aspect of our lives.

It soon became obvious that if we wanted to help spread the Dharma in Norfolk we would have to start in a much more densely populated area. Sona had already been working with other Order members to find properties for a country retreat centre for men— which was also to serve as Bhante's residence—and a public Buddhist centre in Norwich. When activities began at the new centre Sona wanted to be there helping. It was obviously more difficult for me to take an active part in classes in Norwich, and anyway it was time for me to be more adventurous. For some time now we had been considering leading more separate lives. If I was to move, why should I be limited to Norfolk? I knew I didn't want to go back to London. I wanted a pleasant and healthy environment in which to bring up the girls. London was hardly that, and if I went there I might have been tempted to depend too much on my mother—and she on me. There were a number of women Mitras in Brighton, several of whom had children. I wanted to be amongst other mothers, for our mutual support. Vessantara had recently taken over as chairman of the Buddhist Centre there. He was rather on his own in running it, and he was very encouraging when I expressed an interest in moving down.

In retrospect I think there was an element of reaction in my decision to take a look at Brighton. Sona and I were living in quite a bit of tension. We were genuinely struggling to grow spiritually. However, our circumstances could so easily persuade us to sink back, either into enjoying the relative straightforwardness and security of building a home and looking after a family, or into feeling resentful about the limitations we had imposed on ourselves. Perhaps it was partly frustration and resentment at being the one for whom a move was going to be most difficult that motivated me to consider such a big one.

One fine day in the spring of 1976 I packed the car with clothes, nappies, potty, and pushchair, loaded Sundari on to the back seat, safe inside her carry-cot, and strapped two-year-old Shanti into her red plastic child-seat. Then off we rolled in our white Citroën Dyane, stopping for a night with my mother in London to break the journey. I really thought that this was the initial stage of my moving to Brighton with my two young daughters.

As I drove into Brighton I tried to imagine myself living there. By the time I had reached my destination, a whitewashed bay-windowed terraced house sitting on a hill amidst rows and rows of similar dwellings, my sense of excitement had died down. Alone, with my two children, I didn't feel as adventurous as I had done when I'd set off.

Vessantara, whom I hardly knew, welcomed me warmly. The house was centrally heated and carpeted—a pleasant change from my still-being-renovated cottage in the country. We had tea in the kitchen and he told me how things were going in Brighton. There were difficulties and he was badly in need of another Order member to work with. He seemed relieved just to talk with me, even though I found it hard to appreciate much of what was going on. The nearest I'd got to working within a centre situation was keeping the treasurer's books for the activities recently started in Norwich. I did my best to appear interested, offering sympathetic noises now and again. As an Order member I was naturally interested in the functioning of the FWBO, but I hadn't had much experience of it. What, I wondered, would be expected of me if I moved to Brighton? Although I'd thought and talked in terms of wanting to work more directly through a centre, my involvement would actually be quite limited. It struck me that although I would in time benefit the situation, to begin with I would need a lot of support myself.

We sat in the kitchen, inhabiting entirely different worlds. Shanti jiggled about on my lap, impatient for my attention. Vessantara kindly wished me to make myself at home. He'd made the two upstairs bedrooms free for our use. He had no idea that I too was desperate for support, and I didn't let on. What I really needed was another human being who knew what it was like to have young children, who could understand how to help me feel at home, who could help the children to settle in. What I needed was a close woman friend who could understand what I was trying to do. I did what I could to settle in upstairs. Was I seriously considering moving to Brighton, I began to wonder. Why had I come here? Did I really want to move from Great Ryburgh? Did I really have it in me to start anew in a place where I had no friends?

That evening Vessantara was to lead a study group for the women Mitras. He had arranged for it to be held at his house so that I could also attend it. I was pleased to meet the women, one or two of whom I knew slightly, and they were obviously very appreciative of having a Dharmacharini in their midst. I managed to stay with them for about half an hour, and then I heard the sound of a baby crying, so I excused myself to attend to Sundari. I didn't mind too much as I'd hardly taken part in the discussion, and I had decided that on this visit I must be careful to put the children first. But it was a shame. I comforted Sundari and, when I realized that it was not going to be a quick job, resigned myself to not going back into the group. Shanti had woken up too so I brought her through to sleep in my bed. What was I doing? I felt so despondent and alone. I hadn't come simply to attend to my children. And yet, what had I expected? What had I imagined? What had I hoped for? Had I hoped for things to be sud-denly, miraculously different? Had I hoped to feel 'at home' as soon as I'd arrived? Had I hoped to be looked after and appreciated? Was I really prepared for the reality of leaving home taking the children with me?

The following day Vessantara told me that he needed to talk to a Mitra about some matter. Peter and his wife, Jenny, lived in a lodge cottage just outside Brighton. Jenny had been considering becoming a Mitra, but at the moment the couple were on the verge of disillusion-ment with the FWBO. Vessantara thought it might be a good idea if I went to visit them with him. I could drive him there, I could meet Jenny, and it would be an outing for us. He telephoned to see whether we could call in that morning. Yes, they would be in, and we were invited to stay for lunch.

It must have been early spring as I didn't have any really warm winter clothes with me. I threw an ugly old waterproof coat—one I'd borrowed from my mother just in case—into the car. I had adapted too quickly to the warmth of Vessantara's centrally-heated town house and now, on entering the Spartan, stone-floored lodge, I could have kicked myself for not being more suitably attired. I could hardly go and get my coat from the car. And I was too shy and embarrassed to ask to borrow a cardigan. I hoped Sundari was all right in her carry-cot on the cold, draughty floor. There was an Aga in the room but, although it was alight, it was extremely inefficient and the kettle took ages to boil. I shivered in my thin jumper and jiggled Shanti about on my knee.

Vessantara discussed his business with Peter. Jenny threw in a few words now and again, but I couldn't even pretend to be interested. And if she wanted to talk to me about her reservations concerning 'women and the FWBO', she would have to make the first move. I couldn't think about much beyond keeping warm and wondering how long my daughters would last before they made very obvious signs of boredom, hunger, or misery. Eventually someone suggested we go for a bit of a walk round the estate. I brightened up at the prospect—it would give Shanti something to do, although she wasn't very keen on walking—and it would probably be warmer outside. At least I could put my coat on.

Shanti didn't want to use the toilet before we set off so I zipped her up in her two-sizes-too-big blue anorak and wrapped Sundari in her blanket. We were going to walk around the edges of the fields; Peter thought we could probably manage it. It had been raining so the ground was quite muddy. My shoes weren't very suitable and they began to weigh me down as the wet brown mud clung to them. I lagged behind, slowed up by mud and daughters, too far away to keep up with the adult conversation. And then Shanti wanted a wee. I was a bit annoyed with her for not having heeded my request before we left the house. With Sundari in my arms I couldn't help her in the complicated operation of pulling clothes up and down in order for her to relieve herself. I told her she'd have to wait and I walked on. But she couldn't wait for long. First she sulked, and then she began insisting that she was desperate. My irritation with the whole situation was suddenly let loose. Poor little Shanti, I took it all out on her. Somehow I hung on to Sundari as I bent down to manoeuvre the two-sizes-too-big anorak and undo Shanti's trousers. But I was so cross with her that she wet herself before I could lift her up into the appropriate position. I was so fed up I smacked her—then immediately regretted it and felt awful. She already had a bit of a cold; now she would have to walk on with wet knickers, tights, and trousers. I hadn't brought any spare clothes with me and there was little chance of drying her out back at the house.

The others eventually noticed how far away we were and Vessantara came back and offered to carry Sundari for me. My load was lightened and I gave Shanti more attention as we trudged on round the fields. Eventually we returned to the house, which was initially a relief. Sundari was hungry, but before I could deal with her I had to peel Shanti's wet clothes off. I hung them above the Aga even though there was no likelihood of them drying out.

I'd been looking forward to a warming lunch, but Peter and Jenny were macrobiotic, and their thin miso soup and cold rice salad didn't do much to warm up one's insides. Shanti was cold and miserable and wouldn't eat anything. I longed to go home.

Sona Leaves Home

I had visited Brighton imagining that a move there might constitute a literal Going Forth for me, a leaving behind of my familiar home. But I wasn't ready for so drastic a change.

When the girls were settled for the night Sona and I would sit round the old smoking stove—which had travelled with us from Cambridge for sentimental value, although we swore that it could be efficient — and sometimes we would talk about our future. We were ready to take another step; in fact, we needed to. We both wanted to be more actively engaged in the work of the FWBO, and to revitalize our efforts to be less dependent on one another. With the centre in Norwich, and Padmaloka, the men's retreat centre, nearby, it was obvious where Sona's direction lay. Mine was not so clear. Perhaps Sona should at least spend more time at Padmaloka, live there during the week, and come 'home' to Great Ryburgh at weekends. It wasn't a terribly satisfactory arrangement for me. I had no real friends in the village. There was Veronica at the old farm, who was always busy making bread and cheese and tending her vegetables. She had a little boy Shanti's age. And then there were our old dope-smoking friends, Pete and Vida, living at Gateley, a couple of miles away. They still weren't interested in meditation and Buddhism. But despite the unsatisfactoriness of it, we had to do something. We couldn't wait until everything was right. If one of us could be more engaged in a centre and community, that would be better than continuing to live as we were.

So Sona was to go and I would stay at home looking after the house and children. I knew I would be lonely, but what else could we do? We had taken upon ourselves the task of transformation, of realizing our human potential and encouraging others to do likewise; but we weren't making a great deal of progress in the Norfolk countryside. Perhaps life for our neighbours, in spite of the hard work involved in growing vegetables, was too comfortable for substantial change to be seriously contemplated. Having concluded that the task would be more effectively tackled from Norwich or Padmaloka, all the other Buddhists around, except for Sulocana, had moved. Now Sona would be joining them. How could I hold him back just because I hadn't yet found a better situation for myself? Anyway I had to admit that when he was at home all day he could get on my nerves, and I had enough to do looking after two children without having to look after him as well. Yes, I wanted him to go.

On Monday morning he drove off in the car. I lifted the girls up so that they could wave to him. They had no notion that this was the start of their daddy leaving home. It was quite usual for them to wave him off. He would be back soon, and anyway they had me. I put on a brave face and kept myself busy. There was still plenty to do in the house and garden, and the girls often needed attention. It was by no means the first time I'd been alone, but it was different now. It was the beginning of a new way of life—one in which Sona and I would be more separate, more independent of each other. By the second day I'd had enough. I was thoroughly miserable. What on earth was I doing trying to live alone with two young children and without a husband? Stuck out in the countryside, which I couldn't enjoy because it was all farmland and I couldn't push the pram across the fields. And the house still needed so much doing to it. I felt desperately lonely—I wanted Sona to come back, just for one night. Perhaps if I could talk with him it would help me to carry on. I kept going throughout the morning—it was only a few days until the weekend. Surely I could last until then? I couldn't. I was going to phone him up and talk to him. I gathered up some coins, manoeuvred the pram out of the spare room, through the front door, down the muddy path where the drains were still unfinished, and out into the road. I gathered up the girls and piled them into the pram. We set off for the village and the telephone box.

My heart was pounding as I pushed the pram down past the new bungalow and the old farm with the pink house opposite jutting into the road, and then up through the long, straggling village towards the shop, beyond which was my destination. Couldn't I keep going a bit longer? How pathetic of me to want Sona to come back so soon. What would I say to him, and what would I say if it wasn't him who answered? What would they think of me? I left the girls in the pram and went inside the booth, trembling. What if he wouldn't come back? His friends would probably encourage him not to. I didn't want to ask, but my desperation drove me on. Ratnapani answered. He sounded sympathetic. Sona wasn't available just then, could he take a message? My voice quivered as I told him that I wanted Sona to come home. And then I cried.

A Visitor

One evening, after Sona had been at Padmaloka for a week or so, I heard a knock at the door. The children were in bed, it was dark, and I was sitting in the front room reading. Just occasionally one of our neighbours from the old farm had called at this hour, but it was very unusual. The knock came again, and I thought I'd better go and see who was there. The back door was half glazed so before I opened it I could see that my visitor was a stranger—a heavy-looking, dark-bearded man. With a mixture of fear and curiosity I opened the door. Did I own a little ginger and white cat, he asked with concern. With some relief I told him it didn't belong to me, but, as he proceeded to tell me the story of how he'd nearly run it over, I knew that this was just an excuse to call. I thought I recognized him as coming from one of the houses beyond us on the other side of the road. He looked a fairly harmless sort of fellow, but he had the cheek to comment on the fact that my husband was away—and would I like some company? I don't think I was actually rude as I sent him packing, in fact I was probably quite friendly, but the incident disturbed, annoyed, and worried me. It also in some way excited me. I suppose it was quite flattering to have an admirer, however crude, when I now only had a part-time husband. However, it was some time before I stopped feeling nervous in the evenings, and suspicious if ever a car drew up nearby.

Women's Mysteries

I walked at the edge of the group—a small gathering of women Mitras. As we walked along I caught snatches of an animated conversation. The subject was the stringent conditions the Buddha had laid down to Mahaprajapati for the admission of women to the Order. The talk was intense, as though there were some mystery that needed to be unravelled, as though the key to the mystery or the answer to a question had been hidden and we now had to search for it. I strained my ears to follow the gist of the conversation. Presumably, as a woman, it must be relevant to me. I felt a bit left out—too naïve perhaps to appreciate the mystery.

On another occasion, once I was ordained, I walked through Hampstead Heath with a small group of Dharmacharinis. Again I walked at the edge. I didn't understand the concerns which seemed to weigh so heavily on their minds. Why, in particular, were so few women being ordained? I thought it was quite obvious, but I didn't say so—I thought maybe I was being too simplistic.

I tried to educate myself by reading about Women's Mysteries—the moon, menstruation, and a symbiotic relationship with Mother—but I was none the wiser.

We became very conscious of references in the Buddhist Scriptures to women and their inferiority in comparison to men. The offending passages were often avoided, or the terminology changed, because we might be discouraged. It seemed we avoided the basic issue, adding to the mystery rather than solving it.

I took note of what Bhante said on the subject. He told us not to over-identify with being women. He, like the Buddhist tradition, regarded women generally as being at something of a disadvantage, at least at the start of spiritual life, in comparison with men. He gave the example of running a race, in which the woman began with a handicap. He spoke of women as being more bound to the biological. Well, this all made absolute sense to me, tied down as I was by the two products of my womb, my concern for their well-being, and with maintaining a home for them and for me.

A Rare Specimen

Mike, a lecturer in philosophy at the University of East Anglia, had become involved in the movement through Sona's yoga classes. He was very keen to meet a woman Order member and so Sona invited him, along with another university friend, to supper one evening at Great Ryburgh. I felt rather proud that I was to be examined as a rare specimen, and yet afraid that he would discover little to impress him. I suppose I thought he was just interested to see how I would shape up intellectually. But he didn't give me a hard time after all; in fact, he praised my apple-crumble.

Teresa, the girlfriend of one of Mike's students, also wanted to meet a woman Order member. Once again I was on show, this time on a boat on the river, an outing for a group of Norwich Friends. Later Mike asked me what my impression of her was. I hesitated, thinking this was his opportunity to discover how unperceptive I was. But before I could say it myself he answered for me, 'She talks a lot, doesn't she!'

When the Centre was started in Norwich I wanted to help. I couldn't get in to classes but I could act as a long-distance treasurer. I carefully transferred all the figures from Devamitra's scraps of paper into my new hard-backed account book. But after a while I found that my job had become an onerous one. In spite of Devamitra's assurances that it was helpful to him, it exaggerated my sense of isolation to be working in such an abstract way.

But now here was Teresa, specifically wanting more contact with a Dharmacharini. There was already one woman Mitra in Norwich. She had moved to Norfolk from London to live in a caravan with one of Sulocana's sons. Dhammadinna suggested that if the two of them could get to Great Ryburgh, I could study with them. I had hardly studied in a group myself and yet my Kalyana Mitra was exhorting me to lead one.

Sometimes they came out on the bus and sometimes they cycled the twenty-five miles from Norwich to Great Ryburgh. They always stayed overnight. They seemed to be very happy to talk about Lizzie's beautiful crocheted garments, her up and down love affair, or Teresa's all-consuming project—the new wholefood shop. We probably could have spent the entire evening in this way, and sometimes we did.

Almost There

When Sundari was a year old I left her and Shanti with Sona and my mother and went on the women's winter retreat. It was the first retreat I'd attended since I'd been ordained, and even before that I hadn't been on many.

Sona brought Sundari in and I showed her off on the kitchen table before saying goodbye for a week. What a relief it was to be without children for a while. I could have been quite happy simply being on retreat with no children to attend to. However, as an Order member I now had other responsibilities. The Order members running the retreat would meet up each day to plan the programme and the work to be done, and we would discuss how the retreat was going, and talk a bit about how we ourselves were faring. I was inexperienced in such situations and had little to say for myself. I watched to see how the others worked. I was happiest in the shrine-room, meditating.

Feeling shy and inexperienced, even amongst other Order members, I couldn't relax very easily. Malini befriended me and one day offered to give me a massage. What a treat—so relaxing and sensuous. She won my heart. She told me she wanted to move back into the country. She would grow herbs in the shape of a mandala. I listened to her talk, and encouraged her to think seriously about moving up to Norfolk. My circumstances were quite unsatisfactory; to have another Dharmacharini around would change them dramatically.

Our talk of country living, growing herbs and vegetables, starting a community or perhaps even a retreat centre, attracted attention and interest. Perhaps it wasn't a dream after all; maybe something would come of it. Do, an artist in a pale green and white sweater who had taken to meditation and Buddhism like a duck to water, showed particular interest.

I could only stay for a week of the retreat and then it was back to Norfolk and motherhood for me. I was refreshed and invigorated, ready to review my living situation once again and explore the changes I might make for the better.

In spite of Malini's enthusiasm for moving to Norfolk I wasn't expecting much to come of it. So I was very surprised when I received a phone call to say that she and Do and two others wanted to come and spend a weekend with me; they wanted to look at properties that might be suitable for our country community. I was delighted and nervous at the same time. Could it really be that this was the beginning of a community for me? And now that others were seriously interested, was it what I really wanted? In spite of my apprehensions, I thought it was.

Teresa and Annie had been on the second week of the winter retreat and it was then that plans to start a community had really got going. Annie was very keen. She owned her own house and was prepared to sell it in order to buy a place for the community. So already one major obstacle was apparently overcome. Teresa had been living in Norwich with her boyfriend. She wanted to involve herself more deeply in the movement and the spiritual life and, when her boyfriend moved out to live in a men's community, she was eager to experiment with a women's community. Back home, after the retreat, she had been scouring the estate agents for suitable properties.

On that occasion we found nothing that was worth following up. We did, however, get a more realistic picture of our project. The countryside was rather bleak at that time of year and the empty houses hardly inviting. I tried not to think of the comfort of my own home, and kept reminding myself of the isolation I experienced there. By the end of the weekend Do had decided that this move was not for her. Malini, on the other hand, was planning to move in with Teresa so that she would be on the spot to look at properties and build up connections with us in Norfolk. Annie was still prepared to buy.

I was already in the habit of staying regularly overnight with Teresa. I would go into Norwich to lead a study group at her house for the handful of women Mitras, or to attend an Order meeting whilst she baby-sat for me. I would fix up a makeshift cot for Sundari, and Shanti would sleep with me on a mattress on the floor. Once Malini had moved in there was no longer a spare room and what had already been a rather cumbersome, though rewarding, business became more difficult and less worthwhile. I had been enjoying deepening my friendships with both Teresa and Malini when I saw them alone. But when I joined them now at Recreation Road, my hands full with two little girls, I felt in the way and unable to share in the sense of community that I imagined they were developing.

The search for a property continued. The plan was now definitely to establish a retreat centre for women, not just a community. I had to consider carefully whether it would be wise for me still to be involved. It wouldn't be ideal, but for me personally it would almost be a Pure Land compared with living alone out at Great Ryburgh. And the project itself would benefit from having two Dharmacharinis rather than only one—even with the addition of children.

However, it wasn't easy for me to remain inspired about my own part in the project. I could think of many reasons why I shouldn't be involved, but the others encouraged me to put them aside and to look forward to what we could create. Once Teresa and I looked at a property that was much too big and grand for our needs. It fired Teresa with a vision for the future: one day we would need such a place for a retreat centre—and indeed, some seventeen years later, she has been the main force behind procuring just such a place. But I was too bound up with children complaining of the cold to get excited about the potential of this neglected mansion. My vision wasn't strong enough for me to overcome my dismay at the idea of living once again, with young children, on a building site.

But Not For Me

Street Farm at Aslacton was rather quaint, but didn't immediately strike me as suitable for our purposes. Annie, however, had fallen in love with it and so we went back for a second look to consider it more seriously. It had charm and it had potential—I'm afraid I was reminded of the unrealized potential of Abhirati. The house itself was not large but would probably hold a small community. The place was more of a smallholding than a farm, with a few acres of land, some greenhouses which Malini was most interested in, and a complex of barns which with a little imagination seemed ripe for conversion into retreat facilities.

Bhante came out to see what sort of a place we were considering acquiring. He was obviously very interested in the surrounding properties—quite as much it seemed as the one we proposed buying—and remarked on there being a couple of empty houses for sale just across the road, as though we should be thinking in terms of buying them as well. He seemed quite happy for us to go ahead.

So at last our dream was beginning to take real shape. But I was still feeling quite apprehensive—and then I found myself faced with a challenge. Someone else was starting to question my involvement. Malini was having second thoughts about the appropriateness of having children at a retreat centre, but more specifically she was worried that I might expect her to act as father to my children and even as husband to myself. Apparently she had lived with a woman and her children before and that was the role expected of her. She didn't want to repeat that situation. But I had absolutely no desire to regard her in that way. I was shocked, hurt, and angry. The girls had a perfectly good father already, and although he wouldn't be living with us, he had no intention of abandoning his daughters. I had already proved myself capable of managing as a part-time single parent. It wasn't a husband I was looking for—it was spiritual friendship.

Malini came to the conclusion that if I was to be a member of the community then she could not be. It was either her or me. I didn't know what to say—I felt as though some sort of battle had been declared. Should I simply back off or did I consider my position to be worthy, for myself and others, of defending? There was no simple answer. I was tempted to back off, but I received some strong encouragement not to. My brother spoke with great feeling. Such an opportunity had come my way, my chance to fulfil the duties I had as a mother within a more fully engaged spiritual context. How could I let that opportunity go by without a fight?

I summoned up all the determination I could muster and went to talk with Annie at her home in London. I knew she was keen for me to be involved, but at what cost? I'd thought that with her support I was home, as it were. But our meeting was a bit tense. It transpired that she was concerned about the project if Malini was no longer participating in it. And perhaps, after all, it wouldn't be appropriate to have children at a retreat centre. Reluctantly, Teresa was wondering too. The matter had to be decided between the four of us. Poor Teresa and Annie were faced with a difficult task, for in effect the decision rested with them.

After the usual lengthy negotiations, the purchase of Street Farm was almost complete and it would soon be ready to move in to. The four of us met up at Recreation Road. I hovered nervously whilst Teresa, chatting away, made the tea, waiting for Annie to arrive. When the doorbell rang I wanted the ground to swallow me up. Now was the time for us to come to a decision and basically it was up to Annie and Teresa to choose between Malini and me. None of us wanted to be in the position we were in. We all knew what the outcome would be, but we had to state it, together. Annie and Teresa didn't want to lose either of us, but a choice had to be made. Malini, being the more obviously able-bodied of the two of us, was vital to the project and so she was to remain.

I had pushed myself beyond my own inclinations to be a part of this project and finally there was no point in pushing any more. For me, at least, it wasn't to be. Perhaps in the end I felt some relief. My hurt dissolved enough for me to be able to offer my services on the day the others moved in.

How different, I wonder, would my life have been if I had been a member of that community? I was left with a bruise but no regrets. And later I was glad not to have lived through some of the difficult times the others experienced there.

It is hard to live in the world
And hard to live out of it.
It is hard to be one among
many.

five

Another Experiment

From out of the blue I received a letter from Dominique, a French girl I'd met on retreat a couple of years before. She was living in France, now had a baby, and wanted to participate more effectively in the FWBO. Did I know of any family community that she could join? No I didn't—if I had, I might have been living in it myself. My mind began to race around. When the girls were in bed I would sit under the stairs—my favourite place for contemplation—and imagine living with another woman Buddhist, one who also had a child. I hardly knew Dominique. What I particularly remembered of her was that, when we were cooking together on retreat, she told me to cut the potatoes up smaller than I had done.

Wanting to be nearer the Centre and to take part in some of its activities, I had already begun to consider moving to Norwich. Should I invite Dominique to join me? Could this be the beginning of a community? I wrote back to her and she was interested.

Having decided that I should move to Norwich, I wondered how I could do so. I wasn't sure I wanted to sell the house in Great Ryburgh, especially as I didn't know what I would be giving it up for. And then the blue sky presented me with another opportunity. It just so happened that Mike, the philosopher, wanted to spend some time in the country in order to concentrate on his writing. He owned a small terraced house in Norwich and suggested swapping with me. We met up, looked over one another's houses, and very quickly agreed to exchange for about a year. It was a friendly and easy arrangement; we would leave most of our belongings behind for each other's use, and we would be prepared to swap back again at any time if for some reason things didn't work out.

In the course of correspondence with Dominique I found that her position was complicated. Her boyfriend, the father of her child, did not want her to come to England, and neither did her parents. In fact they thought she was getting caught up in some sort of brainwashing sect like the Moonies, who were infamous at the time. She assured me that she was still coming, however, and so, a little nervously, I fixed a date with Mike for the move.

Sona borrowed a van from Padmaloka and helped me take all I needed from Great Ryburgh to 104 Glebe Road, Norwich.

We fixed up Sundari's cot in the little room where the girls were to sleep. My room was the biggest, at the front, overlooking the road and a stretch of terraced houses. There was a double mattress on the floor. I was going to miss my bed. Someone had told me that the room was haunted. Although I tried to dismiss such thoughts, I couldn't help feeling a little wary. I wished Sona would stay, but we'd decided to observe celibacy for three months, to give me space to settle into my new life. I felt empty and lonely that night, though the next morning there was plenty to do to keep me busy.

I still hadn't heard exactly when Dominique would be arriving. I began to arrange the house as I wanted it; it was hard to settle into and enjoy my new home when such an important element was yet to come.

I received a frantic phone call from Dominique. She had been shocked to discover that her boyfriend had been having an affair. Not only that—and this was what seemed to shock her most—it was with a woman she disliked! But the worst thing was that her parents, still under the impression that she was being brainwashed, had apparently kidnapped Steve, her little boy. She would simply come whenever she could, and she asked me to be ready to meet her at Heathrow at short notice. Little did I imagine at the time that this dramatic beginning to our life together was a taste of what was to come.

About three weeks after my arrival in Norwich I went down to London, left the girls with my mother, and made my way to Heathrow. I arrived in good time to find that the plane was delayed. I waited, and waited, and waited. Would she really, finally, be coming to live with me? I wasn't even sure that I'd recognize her. A tall slim woman with long dark hair, carrying a baby boy, appeared. Suddenly there was a smile of recognition and we greeted each other with relief. Dominique talked excitedly of her escape from France. I listened in quiet amazement, trying to piece together what had happened. She was a very lively, energetic woman, and she appeared to be on good form in spite of her recent traumatic adventures.

We managed about six months together. From the start I found that I couldn't rely on Dominique's commitment to living with me. She was still very caught up with her boyfriend and hadn't thought through how she would maintain her involvement with him. She got extremely upset as she discovered more and more of the intrigue surrounding his affair. Rather naïvely I thought that maybe this was her opportunity to make a break with him and get on with her life in England. But romantic relationships are never that simple.

To begin with it was a real pleasure to have another adult around to work and play with. We managed to co-operate with one another in the running of the household. I was irritated by some of her little ways, but I usually put up with them. I suppose she might have had some reason to complain of me—although I wasn't aware of any!

We could easily baby-sit for each other and so we regularly attended classes at the Centre. And occasionally we would call in a baby-sitter and go out for an evening together, feeling sixteen again.

Dominique was a very intense woman. Once the crisis with her boyfriend had calmed down a bit, she was ready to immerse herself in the Dharma. She wanted to be ordained. She thought she should be. She experienced some strange states that both worried her and convinced her that she was well on her way to Enlightenment. Led on by her mystically inspired intuition, she became obsessed with a Tibetan text she had come across. At all costs she had to get a minder for Steve so that she could devote herself to its study. I didn't offer. Our little community wasn't working out. Dominique, impatient with the FWBO's tardiness in recognizing her spiritual maturity, was now bent on doing her own thing. She had a touch of madness about her. It was a strain living with her, and I felt for poor little Steve, who was being somewhat neglected.

The Last Straw

The 1977 Order Convention was to take place in Sussex. I managed to persuade my sister and her husband to take a holiday in Norwich and look after my children for part of the time I was to be away. Dominique had arranged a visit to France then, but she planned to be back in order to be with the girls when my sister left.

Slightly uneasy about the transition between baby-sitters, I decided to return home in the middle of the Convention to make sure that all went smoothly.

When I arrived home there was no Dominique. This was the last straw. I'd had enough. I couldn't bear the intensity, the disruption, and the uncertainty of living with her any longer. I would have to ask her to leave.

For the time being I was determined to get back to the Convention. Vida, my dear old friend Vida, was my only hope. I knew her life was somewhat complicated at the time, but I could at least ask. Asking, however, was not so easily done. She didn't have a phone and she lived twenty-five miles away. I telephoned her neighbour who, luckily, was at home. Then all I could do was wait, hoping that a message would get through. The following day Vida arrived in her car to pick up the girls.

Back on the train to Sussex, having been afraid I wouldn't be returning to the Convention, I breathed a sigh of relief. How would one survive without friends? But I also felt a bit guilty at having rather frantically disposed of my children. And I felt both upset and relieved thinking of Dominique and how our experiment of living together was now going to have to end.

Meeting Needs

There were not enough Kalyana Mitras for the growing number of Friends wanting to become Mitras and so Mitra Convenors were introduced at each centre, one for men and one for women. They were responsible for making sure that the spiritual needs of the Mitras were met. They would watch over the Mitras in a more general way than the Kalyana Mitras had done, making sure that they had adequate facilities and opportunities for deepening their spiritual practice. They would especially encourage them in their practice of ethical behaviour, meditation, the development of spiritual friendship, and study of the Dharma. Dhammadinna became the Overall Convenor of Women Mitras and I took on responsibility for the women in Norwich. My work for the movement was now more defined and I even had a sort of boss, my own Kalyana Mitra, a friend I respected and looked up to. Albeit at a distance, I could report to her, turn to her, and when necessary be spurred on by her.

Now that I was living in Norwich I was able to lead a study group regularly each week for the Mitras, and we were usually undisturbed by my daughters. I made myself available to be visited by any women who especially wanted to talk with a Dharmacharini. Sometimes I enjoyed getting to know my visitors, but sometimes, being rather too much of a good listener, I found myself getting tired and irritated as they talked, not with me, but only at me. Then I wished there were someone closer at hand who would make sure *my* spiritual needs were being met, or just someone who was obviously interested in me, who would give me a bit of attention.

I Picked Up a Handful of Toys and
Flung Them Around the Room

Shanti went to play school in the local Church hall. She was quiet and shy, and made friends only very slowly. I didn't help, not being interested in making conversation with the other mothers.

I pushed the pushchair, laden with Sundari and a big bag of washing, down the road, up the hill past the park and on to the shopping complex. Once the washing was in the machine we wheeled a trolley around FineFare, where in spite of my list I was always in a daze when confronted with so much choice. Oh, what a tedious life this could be!

Although relieved that Dominique had gone, I didn't really enjoy living on my own again. The community at Street Farm wasn't developing as Teresa had hoped, and my spirits lifted when she moved back into Norwich—especially when she found a room nearby. When she got ill with mumps she moved in with me so that I could look after her. I would have liked her to carry on living with me. She wanted to start up a new community in Norwich. I wondered if we could start one together, but she wasn't sure about living with children.

She told me about the time she worked in India, and said how she would like to return some time as a nun. I was impressed by her enthusiasm, but couldn't appreciate her ardent attraction, inexplicable even to herself, for a shaven head and robe.

It was nearly time for Mike and me to return to our own homes. I had decided that I wanted to continue living in Norwich so I began looking around for a house to buy.

Whilst I was looking I was told of an empty house in Clarence Road that was to let. The rent was low and it was a large building, with big rooms and plenty of them. It would be nice to have all that space after being squashed between neighbours in a small terraced house. However, I had also seen a property I was interested in buying. It *was* a small terraced house but it was very well situated. It stood in a private, unmade cul-de-sac called Lollard's Road, at the foot of which was the river. The station was five minutes away by foot and to get into the centre of town I would have a delightful walk through the Cathedral Close. There were only two bedrooms, so the girls would have to share, and there wasn't much of a garden. But the positioning was perfect. I knew that in any of the other places I'd looked at I would have felt hemmed in within rows and rows of identical houses, and isolated through being so far away from the centre of town.

I went back to Great Ryburgh to put the house up for sale and start proceedings for buying the one in Lollard's Road. As a contingency plan I took on the lease of the house in Clarence Road, letting Teresa move in, with the proviso that if there were any setbacks in my negotiations I would be moving back. She obviously didn't really think it would come to that. Unfortunately it did, and my reappearance unwittingly destroyed the little community that she had been nurturing. Feeling her efforts had been thwarted, Teresa decided to go to London. I had hoped she would stay, my one real friend in Norwich, and we both felt hurt. Avril had only wanted a taste of community life and was ready to return home to her husband, but Beryl stayed on with me. I could now pick up the threads of my life in Norwich, resume my study group and the class I helped with at the Centre, and start Shanti at nursery and Sundari at play school.

Living with Beryl didn't work out. She wanted a lot of my attention and sometimes seemed oblivious to the fact that I had two little girls clamouring for it as well. And who was going to listen to me? One evening I was trying to get the girls to put their toys away and go upstairs for their bath. Beryl chattered on, and more and more toys were covering the floor. No one seemed to notice my frazzled state. I lost what little patience I had. 'Why won't anyone listen to me?' I screamed as I picked up a handful of toys and flung them around the room. Later I felt so bad at having lost control like that. I turned to my friend, Vida, and indulged in a little dope-smoking—a pleasant but fleeting respite. I turned to Sona, wanting him to make everything all right, but I knew really that he couldn't.

One day I was late leaving to collect Shanti from her nursery. Sundari wasn't helping matters and I impatiently hurried her through the front door as I struggled with the pushchair. I didn't notice that she was running her fingers up and down the edge of the door as I slammed it. It wouldn't shut and, annoyed, I was about to try again when Sundari yelled and I saw her crushed finger. Thoroughly shaken by what I'd done I wrapped a bandage around the damaged limb and then, really late now, we set off once again for the nursery. Sundari appeared to be rather proud as she showed Shanti the reason for her being the last to be collected. Worried that the finger might be broken I took the girls straight to the hospital. The fact that the nurse had the same surname as us cheered Sundari up, and she went off quite happily for an X-ray. In spite of Nurse Fricker's careful bandaging, using the adjacent finger as a splint, Sundari's little finger is still bent today.

Beryl moved into a flat round the corner, and I lived on for a while at Clarence Road. If I was to commit myself to attending classes at the Centre I needed a regular baby-sitter. My advertisement in the local post office was answered by the most wonderful baby-sitter I'd ever had or was ever to come across. Her rates were very reasonable. She didn't mind that we had no television. Almost as soon as she walked in the door she would start playing hide-and-seek with the girls. She told them crazy stories and brought her high-heeled shoes round for them to wear. When Terry was with them I had no qualms about leaving my daughters.

But all good things come to an end, and Terry eventually got married and moved away. Several baby-sitters came and went before I was satisfied with another. And even then I would sometimes go out leaving a little girl with tears in her eyes, pleading with me not to go.

I Used to Dream

Sitting under the stairs at Great Ryburgh, eating bread and syrup, I used to dream of a better way to live. I longed for the company, the understanding, the support, and the stimulation of other women Buddhists who, like me, had children.

And even when I was living in Norwich surrounded by families, or single mothers and their children, who had gradually made their way up from the big metropolis, I wasn't satisfied. I had what I'd longed for but it wasn't enough. In spite of my own experience, and the attempts of others to live together, I continued to dream of a community.

It was a long while before I finally gave up the idea of living with other women and children. It was usually when I'd been away on retreat that the idea would nag at me again. I would come home and, alone with my children, feel confined, restricted, lacking in stimulation and close friendship.

A stream of Buddhist parents, all seeking a better way to live, trickled in and out of Norwich. Ray and Jaya had at last decided to move from London, Do too, now with a young son. John and Jenny came, and André arrived in her Mini with two children and whatever belongings she'd managed to fit around them, leaving her husband behind. Verne came over from New Zealand, leaving *her* husband at Gatwick, and Daphne and Dave came from Ireland. Annie, out at the farm, now had a baby, and there were several indigenous Friends who were mothers too.

Jenny and Jaya were the first of the women to arrive. They both wanted to be ordained. I felt spoilt when I went to visit them in their new homes just outside Norwich. Our children played together and we could talk—getting to know one other, commiserating with and stimulating one another. And it was good to be in the country again. Before I'd known them very long I was leaving my girls with them for a night or two so that I could get away to an Order weekend. Sometimes I felt I was taking advantage of these other parents. I relied on them, knowing I wouldn't be looking after their children to the extent they looked after mine. I tried not to feel guilty about not returning favours.

After the initial relief and delight of having other mothers around, I began to wonder why I didn't feel as though my dream had come true. It wasn't easy to be free of children. We might manage a few minutes of uninterrupted conversation and then one child or another would appear demanding attention. Even when my own children were off my hands at school, there were always others around. And even when they weren't around we still had the rest of the domestic business to attend to. Perhaps, in spite of the attempts some of us had made, we hadn't gone far enough. We talked of a Buddhist school. For a while I was enthusiastic, and then I had to admit that I no longer saw teaching as my vocation. I didn't want to be surrounded by children all the time, no matter how disapproving I was of the education my own were receiving.

I heard of a large house in the country that had recently been vacated by a Sufi community and was now available to let. I began to dream again. I gathered up a few of my friends who might, however remotely, be interested, and suggested we go out and look at it. It was a lovely house, similar in style to Abhirati, but it wasn't rotting; it had been well cared for. How many of us would it hold? Could we afford it? We'd be reliant on cars. What would we do all day out in the country? Could we still work in Norwich, get to classes? It would have to be a self-supporting project. We might get a bit isolated.

Although we were all very taken with the house, there wasn't a lot of enthusiasm for the project—indeed, we hadn't even formulated one.

Many a night had I lain awake, designing the ideal community, imagining the space we'd need, imagining a fine old building with outhouses and extensive grounds. Now that it stood before me I couldn't let this opportunity slip too quickly through my fingers; I was forced to do some serious thinking. I was the only Dharmacharini in Norwich. Was it fair to move away from the Centre to take on a venture that would require all my energy? I had to admit that on my own I didn't have the vision or faith necessary to take others and our children with me. Judging from experience, I reckoned a community should begin when the children were very young, and even then it would take serious commitment to be able to live harmoniously together. It would also be essential to include a number of women who weren't mothers, so as not to be dominated by children. I came to the conclusion that it was too late for me to attempt such a life-style, and I went ahead with the purchase of the house in Lollard's Road.

Even after I'd settled into my chosen abode, I would still return from retreats feeling confined, restricted, in need of deeper friend-ship. And my mind would wander off once again. Verne was think-ing of buying somewhere in Norwich. Maybe we could live together? She was all for it and encouraged me to look at a house we'd seen for sale. Peering into the empty, neglected rooms, I thought of my own home with the sunshine streaming into it, and became more realistic. How would her husband figure in our proposed new life together? Could I really bear to live with more children—and boys at that—now that mine were growing up a bit? The house was hardly big enough and there were too many question marks. If I were to move again I would want to feel convinced that it was my last move for many years to come.

Several years later I nearly pulled it off. A friend was wanting to sell his house. It had previously been the home of a community and was situated very near to Lollard's Road. He was willing to sell it to me at a very low price, which would mean I would hardly need to raise any money after selling my own home. It wasn't my ideal house. The lay-out was awkward, the bathroom cold and damp, it stood right on a busy road, and had only a yard for a garden. But the rooms were spa-cious and we could have someone—or two—living with us. The girls fell in love with the attic room with its polished wood floor and green blinds, which I'd had an eye on for myself. They argued as to whose room it should be and went wild running up and down the three flights of stairs. With them getting bigger and our house seeming to get smaller I had, with a bit of help from my parents, already been considering either extending our house or trying to find somewhere with more room.

Perhaps Do, and her little boy Danny, could live with us? We talked it over tentatively. Do and I were much keener than the children were.

If I wanted a larger house in the same area this, it seemed, was my only chance. A little nervously, I decided to go ahead. However, as far as a community was concerned, I began to admit that I really wasn't up to living with another child, especially if it was going to be against my own children's wishes.

Rather too quickly I accepted an offer on my house and embarked on the lengthy process of selling it and buying the new one. My friend was in a hurry to sell and when I lost my buyer, I couldn't meet his deadline. I was worn down by the whole business, and my desire for the new house was not strong enough to make me plead for more time.

Having been prepared to spend money on moving, I now decided to stay where I was and build on an extra room, so that at least we would have more space. With this decision I was sealing our future. No more moves until the girls were ready to leave home. Even so, I still wasn't immune from thinking. And when my daughters were on their way to leaving home I had one last try. Instead of simply wondering, I asked my old friend, Vida, (who by then had long since renounced her old life and been ordained) if she would consider selling her house and buying somewhere with me. I knew what her answer would be—it wouldn't be fair on Jan (her son) to live with even more women—and I knew she was right. But I just had to try—one last time.

A Welcome Prison

I'd been finding life a little difficult. Children under my feet and dry rot appearing for the second time. The kitchen floor would have to be replaced and the living-room floor taken up for inspection.

At the Buddhist Centre I met Michael, who had moved to Norwich from Bristol. He wanted to re-establish his connection with the FWBO. He'd found a job, and a house which he was putting the finishing touches to. When it was ready his wife and son would move in. He was concerned that it should be just right for his wife. He wanted her to be happy in Norwich. He was laying down 'cushionfloor' in the kitchen. She would like that. That night I dreamt I was happily imprisoned in a cushionfloor kitchen with a Michael keeping guard.

If you are filled with desire
Your sorrows swell
Like the grass after the rain.

But if you subdue desire
Your sorrows fall from you
Like drops of water from a
lotus flower.

Letting Go

Sona came and stayed at Lollard's Road to look after the girls whilst I went on retreat out at Aslacton. I was looking forward to the retreat. After my attempt at living with Dominique and Steve, then living back at Great Ryburgh for a while, being thrown together with Beryl, and considering starting a community for women and children in the country, I now felt I had a solid base from which to function. I had made up my mind to live and work in Norwich. I had the support of my own home and I could now apply myself more vigorously to my work without worrying about where or how I was going to live. Over the last few years I had been striving to be more independent of Sona. I hoped this retreat would show me the fruit of my effort. It could be an opportunity to connect more deeply with other women in the movement.

It was the first week-long retreat I'd been on for about eighteen months and only the second I'd supported as an Order member. Almost immediately on arriving I felt myself softening, the strain of the last year or so easing away from my shoulders. I was so happy to be in the company of these other women and to be focusing on spiritual practice: study, meditation, and communication. In such supportive conditions I felt I could relax, and I understood what was meant by 'letting go'. I let go of my home, my children, my struggles, and I experienced myself disorientated but relieved. I loved to be in the shrine-room, and sometimes whilst meditating my whole body would tremble, as if lightening its load.

We were going to make special offerings for the puja—something that symbolized our feeling for the Buddha. I wanted to offer my whole self, I wanted my spiritual aspiration to be held back by nothing. I looked down at my hands and saw the gold ring on my finger. A plain and unobtrusive band of gold, symbol of my bonds, beloved though they were. I slipped it off my finger. It was that that I would offer.

I felt slightly intoxicated. I felt a surge of emotion, of intense love, welling up inside me.

I watched Noel tinkering about with her old blue van. I was fascinated by her. She appeared to me to be a free spirit, without bonds, independent and capable, fearless, at one with nature and the moonlight. I admired her. I wanted to be in her company, to walk and talk in the countryside with her. I felt as though my heart was no longer my own. I wanted to express my love but I was afraid. Where might it lead? In spite of my fears, I could contain my feelings no longer. I picked a flower and self-consciously I offered it to her.

I had let go of too much, too quickly, and now I needed something to hold on to. I directed my full heart towards one person and when she responded, my opened-up world shrank and I was virtually oblivious of anything but her. I felt, however, as though I could conquer the world.

Sona looked pleased to see me when I got home. The girls were in bed and he'd kept supper for me. He'd enjoyed looking after them and thought perhaps he'd try to spend more time with them. I was agitated, he sensed there was something wrong, and eventually I told him, 'I don't want to be married any more.' He was stunned. He could tell that this wasn't simply the next step in our ongoing efforts to be less bound up with one another; something specific had happened. I couldn't bear to see him hurt, I was sorry it was all so abrupt. Had I perhaps thought he might understand, or be sympathetic? I don't know. I was galvanized by the love I felt and the apparent freedom I'd gained, and so I stood my ground. I didn't feel altogether sure of myself, but I was blind to the element of reactive desire in my behaviour.

Looking back I regret what I did. It caused a lot of pain. However, for some time it was the source of a great deal of happiness. I had felt very alone as a mother and a member of the Order. I lived at some distance from London and the main body of Dharmacharinis. I had resigned myself to making the most of the little contact I did have with them at occasional Order weekends, and I tried not to feel envious of their greater opportunity for deepening friendships. I tried hard to be patient and to assure myself that slowly my friendships would strengthen and deepen. And now, suddenly, I had a close woman friend who was a mother too, with whom I could share so much of my life. There was no 'other half' in her life and I was trying to leave mine to do as he pleased.

In my attempts to be more independent of my husband I had tried not to look to him for emotional support. Being of an introverted nature I had, in my attempts to stand more on my own two feet, held back a lot of painful emotion. I now experienced great relief as I freely turned to my friend. There seemed to be no conflict now, no need to hold back from expressing both my dreams and my sufferings. I had broken a sexual taboo and realized how common it was for some erotic feeling to enter into any relationship. I was more confident in myself and had eased further away from projecting on to, and depending on, men. I was enthusiastic to help other women on the spiritual path. And for a while I followed the current trend and 'donned my dungarees'.

Noel was very sincere in her practice of the Dharma. She was always willing to look after my children to enable me to go on retreat. I was aware of an element of exclusivity between us, but all in all I believed our relationship was for the good. Experiencing such warm feeling for my friend led me to be more adventurous with my other friends. It seemed that I was at last breaking away from the strong conditioning which had led me to believe that I could only love, be really open and intimate with, just one person.

I blossomed in the warmth of such intimate friendship. We wrote to each other, went camping with the kids in her old blue van, and talked about a community. I even gave a talk entitled 'Leaving Home Taking the Children with You', which was basically my last substantial attempt to get others interested in a community of women and children. I wanted to encourage other mothers to realize it was possible to go for Refuge and to 'leave home' even whilst maintaining one.

Sona increased his trips abroad, found himself one girlfriend and then another. He saw less of our daughters because it was so uncomfortable for us to be with each other. I didn't like what was happening between us. In spite of the tension he remained my oldest and dearest friend. I tried to listen broad-mindedly when he told me of his escapades. I tried to pretend that I wasn't hurt and jealous. I wished we could discuss more reasonably my view of how his behaviour was affecting the girls. I didn't want them to think of us as divorced, as no longer loving one another. I began to think I might want to be married to Sona after all. As the father of my children and a fellow member of the Order he was bound up in my life. By falling in love with someone else I had estranged him. I had thought I'd taken a positive step, a step away from emotional dependence on him and towards deepening friendships with women. Perhaps to some degree I had, although I began to wonder whether I wasn't simply moving from one marriage into another. If I wanted marriage it would be better to stick with Sona. We were already emotionally entangled, but in the nine years of our married life we'd gone through a great deal in moving towards freeing ourselves. I had become aware of tangles developing with Noel. I wanted to be her friend without all that. She saw my concern for retaining good relations with Sona as my being drawn back into dependence on men, and pulling away from her. I began to realize that what I'd thought of as a harmless element of exclusivity, of selfish love, was now having its effect. Our friendship was in fact already a bit sticky. I had wanted more freedom and clarity in my life but instead I'd got myself into a muddle. I wanted our relationship to change, and I wanted Sona to be my husband—or at least my sexual partner—again.

I had to come to my own decision as to what I wanted. Sona was enjoying his freedom and Noel wouldn't believe that if I went back to him, she and I could remain friends. It was my turn to suffer. I wanted a husband and a friend. Noel proved herself right. I persevered for some time to remain in contact, but she wouldn't respond to my efforts. So I lost my friend and I had to wait patiently for Sona, for although I was fairly confident that he would 'come back to me', he would give me no assurance, and I knew that it now had to be on his terms.

I'm sure that it was very good for me to be kept hanging on. I had come to the conclusion that I was not yet ready to do without the physical and emotional intimacy and all the bonding that went along with a sexual relationship. But for a while, in order to re-establish that intimacy, I had to do without it. A romantic dream that I hadn't realized I had held vanished before my eyes. I had to experience being alone. I had to be 'an island unto myself'. In spite of the pain I experienced I also felt somewhat liberated. I was free for a while from the disturbing business of hope, expectation, and longing, and from the reliance on another for my own happiness. By the time Sona and I renewed our marriage vows, in one sense at least, I felt confident that we were a step closer to dissolving them.

I Didn't Really Mean it!

During Sona's visits abroad, which he had welcomed as a way of avoiding his unfaithful wife, he had begun to think seriously about moving to Sweden, and before I had realized the folly of my ways he had decided to do so.

Having established both business and Buddhist contacts in Sweden, it was soon time for him to live there rather than at Padmaloka. He would return to England once every three months or so and would then spend some time with us. Although we'd managed over the last few years without seeing a great deal of him, now that he would be spending most of his time out of the country we were bound to miss him. It would be hard for the girls to understand that he wouldn't be easily available.

Within the rather bizarre context of maintaining a marriage whilst also trying in some respects to dissolve it, we discussed whether we would be faithful to one another when Sona was in Sweden. I thought that that was what I would prefer, but I wouldn't mind, I said, if he had a fling, so long as I didn't hear about it.

I took the girls with me to visit Sona in the Christmas holidays of 1979. The friend with whom he shared was away, so we had the flat to ourselves. The girls immediately made the place their own. It was good to be together again. I'd found the last few months quite a strain, coming to terms with the fact that Sona no longer lived close by. Sometimes when I put the children to bed they would ask for their daddy. I had to hold back my own tears, ignore my own distress, and comfort them with calm, reassuring words.

There was a little awkwardness to begin with. We'd never before lived together in Sona's home. I felt out of place. We half joked about me and the girls moving to Sweden. There was an English school, and there were already several women attending classes at the Buddhist Centre and needing the attention of a Dharmacharini. I didn't like living so far apart. But we couldn't live together again. And I couldn't forsake the women in Norwich.

Sona proudly showed me his new hat and scarf, knitted for him by an admirer. But why did he then start to act so strangely? He was being cagey about something. He didn't normally hide things from me. I had completely forgotten my own words. I was assuming, as I wanted to, that there was no other woman in his life. I was shocked that he hadn't mentioned her before—before I'd come to stay with him in Sweden. How could he let me even play with the idea of moving here? I was terribly upset. Now a cloud, for me at least, hung over our visit.

Once again, amidst pain and confusion, we had in fact taken a step forward. I had to admit that in saying Sona could have an affair in Sweden but I didn't want to know, I was really saying it's OK in theory but not in practice. I now had to deal with my confused emotions and acknowledge that, although I was upset, I could hardly blame him.

No Strings

We had loosened our hold on each other a little more. It was spring, and sex was in the air. For some time Sona had been encouraging me, in his playful way, to find another man. Of course, he said, it must be someone of whom he approved. He even had someone in mind. It could be a means of relief to us all. I was flattered to hear that his friend had apparently acknowledged an attraction towards me, but I resisted the idea—I was quite happy with one, albeit occasional, man.

Or so I thought. But not only was it spring. Within the movement there was a lot of questioning about conventional morality, and the issue of sex was of particular interest. My attachment to Sona had been loosened. My marriage, it seemed to me, was now fairly steadily and happily dissolving. My apparently broad-minded views had been challenged. What harm was there in experimenting a little more? What harm in indulging in a little pleasure with no strings attached?

By the time I'd made up my mind, my potential lover had shown no sign of approaching me. I decided to take the bull by the horns rather than wait for him to make the first move—for perhaps he never would.

On a couple of occasions I was ready to pop the question but my courage failed me. Finally I decided that if I didn't act quickly I would have to forget about the whole thing. I phoned him up, saying I wanted to meet him as there was something I wanted to talk to him about. Fortunately he didn't ask why I couldn't talk on the phone, and he came to see me that very afternoon.

I took him out for a walk; I couldn't say what I wanted to sitting face to face. As we neared the river I ran out of small talk and simply had to plunge in, so to speak. I stumbled with my words; I thought it must be obvious what I was leading up to, and yet I had to go on and make myself absolutely clear. He said he was game and we fixed a date. There wasn't a lot to say after that. We finished our walk and parted, looking forward to our next rendezvous. I couldn't quite believe what I'd done but I was very glad I'd done it.

I had told Sona in a letter how I had been feeling and what I was thinking of doing. When I told him what I had done he was surprised; I wondered whether he would now feel as enthusiastic about the practice of my sleeping with his friend as he had felt about the theory.

Subhuti and I had formed no ideas as to whether, or how, a relationship might develop. I knew that he really wanted to be celibate. I didn't think I needed another man in my life—just a little sensuous pleasure to keep me going and help me loosen those bonds of attachment. To begin with we took it from date to date. I knew I couldn't rely on him as a lover, but I looked forward to every meeting. We didn't speak a word of love but we grew fonder and fonder of one another. When Subhuti decided, whilst away on retreat, that he must turn again to celibacy, it became clear to us that strings had, after all, taken hold.

And so we went on over the years, falling into and out of each others' arms. Or rather falling into each others' arms only to drag ourselves apart again.

There were a few bumps and bruises with Sona and eventually he and I decided to be monogamous—more or less—but not with each other.

Taking Refuge in the Buddha

There was no water supply at Vajraloka so we had to fetch bucketfuls from the stream. I thoroughly enjoyed the work periods when it was my turn to stand up on the wooden scaffolding, take the buckets which were handed up to me, and pour their contents into the huge plastic butts. I also liked being in the stream, in my wellies, filling up the empty buckets. It was fun too to be part of the chain-gang, swinging empty buckets down towards the stream, and full ones up towards the house.

Vajraloka was an old stone farmhouse with several outbuildings, set on the side of a hill in the Welsh countryside. It was a retreat centre devoted to the practice of meditation.

The shrine-room was magical. A grey stone barn with whitewashed walls and a carpet on the floor. At one end was a slightly larger than life-sized golden Buddha, radiating a steady determination, that inspired me more than any other image I'd come across. He sat cross-legged in meditation posture, and his large hands, placed one on top of the other in his lap, seemed to beckon me on and encourage me to sit in perfect peace as he was doing.

I sat, sometimes in physical pain, within the calm stillness of the shrine-room, and mostly I experienced stillness deep within myself.

We spent a lot of time in silence and it was easy to maintain a meditative state as we went for walks through the fields and the woods, or sat around outside gazing across the valley, watching the clouds pass in the sky, and contemplating the impermanence of things.

I used to walk down to the river at the foot of the valley. I would wander along a muddy pathway, weaving my way around the trees and up and down the steep bank. I recalled how I delighted in wandering along such pathways when I was a child. Sometimes I would stop to gaze at the smooth grey stones lying on the river bed, or the stream of golden light trickling through the overhanging leaves, and the silvery reflection glistening on the ever-moving water. I needed no other pleasure.

One day we were asked to consider whether we had come across a reading from the Buddhist scriptures, or a poem, that could express our mood or experience of the retreat. I had been reading from Bhante's collection of poems, *The Enchanted Heart*, and when I came across one entitled 'Taking Refuge in the Buddha', I knew immediately that that was my choice. Each verse ended with the refrain, 'My place is at Thy feet'. This expression of my teacher's great reverence and devotion for the Buddha struck a deep chord in my heart. I sat on in the shrine-room, alone, reflecting on my good fortune to be in the place I was, sitting at the feet of the Buddha, and living in the presence of a spiritual friend at whose feet I would be happy to remain forever.

Alone in Sweden

Ten years after I was ordained—and five years after Sona had moved to Sweden—I went on my first substantial solitary retreat. I went to Sweden for a month, to stay in the country house of some Friends. Until then I'd only been on my own for up to a week at a time.

The house was familiar as I'd spent a holiday with Sona and the girls there. Since then the attic had been converted into a very spacious living-room and an extra bedroom.

Max and Paleamona took me into town to stock up with provisions. I relied on them to help me decide what and how much I would need for a month. There were a few vegetables in the garden and there was a small shop a short bicycle ride away.

When they had gone, I let myself unwind in the spacious house. I wandered in and out of the rooms, up and down the stairs, and out into the garden. Before me lay an expanse of golden fields. Behind me the forest loomed. I peeped into the gypsy caravan where Shanti and Sundari had spent most of their time.

Max warned me that a cat might come prowling around. It had belonged to them and had disappeared into the forest and turned wild. Sometimes it came back crying for food. They told me to ignore it. Inevitably it came and howled and haunted me in the middle of the night. When it didn't come, I still lay awake wondering if it would. I wished I had befriended it.

I meditated, read, studied the *Satipatthana Sutta,* and went out for long walks or bicycle rides. I cycled through the forest and sat on a granite boulder, gazing across a still, clear lake glistening in the evening sun. Tall pine trees stretched away for miles. I wondered whether I was doing what one should do on a solitary retreat—and how should one feel? I wasn't having any 'experiences'. I tried to be mindful, sometimes I felt a bit frightened, and I often felt lonely. From my upstairs window I watched the cows across the road. When it rained I felt melancholy. I read Ryokan's Zen poetry and looked out to see if the cows minded the rain. Sometimes, on a fine day when I had the window open, I could hear the voices of the children who were staying in the house at the foot of the hill. But their summer was over before mine, and I missed them when they went back to Stockholm.

It slowly dawned on me that I was having an experience. I was experiencing being on my own.

At the end of my retreat I stayed a night in Stockholm. No one answered the doorbell, so I found the key to Sona's flat and let myself in. I dropped my bag in Sona's room and looked around to see if any-one was at home. The curtains in the other bedroom were drawn, as though the inhabitant had gone away. The fridge was almost bare. I was a bit surprised, as Joao, who shared with Sona, had led me to believe he would be around. I was rather disappointed; it was lunchtime and I'd had enough of solitary meals.

After a rather boring lunch I settled into Sona's room, played some music and flicked through a book. A ringing sound started up, com-ing from somewhere in the flat. It kept on going so I ventured out into the hall, the kitchen, and the other room. I discovered an alarm clock, and it did apparently have a purpose. Tucked away in the shadows against the wall was a heap, and it was asleep. I decided to leave both alarm and sleeper to their own devices.

About an hour or so later a tall dark figure, clad in T-shirt and underpants, appeared at my door. Joao couldn't understand why he hadn't woken, and even now he took some time to come to. However, he soon made up for his neglect of me and I was very glad to find that I had a host after all.

I didn't have to wonder what to do with myself for the afternoon. Joao led me off on a crazy sightseeing tour of the city. We sat on a bench, eating chips and chocolate, watching the lights twinkling on the water as we waited for the boat to take us back across the sea. He was so friendly and relaxed, so generous, such delightful company. I don't normally have a lot to say to strangers and in my after-solitary state I was even less talkative than usual. But it didn't matter, Joao talked for the two of us. But why was he so nice to me? Why did I feel so intimate with him? Lulled in his warm, open presence, I almost wished he would take me in his arms.

Back at the house Joao introduced me to Sven, who lived downstairs, and then he set about to cook us all a meal. I was relieved there were now three of us!

I telephoned Sona, who was then in England, to check that he was going to meet me at Heathrow. He couldn't after all—he was spending a few days with Ulrika. I felt hurt, and then disturbed to realize that I still wasn't happy that he had a girlfriend. I wanted to be the only woman in his life, even though he was no longer the only man in mine.

Early the following morning Joao took me to the airport. I was still feeling rather miserably stirred up after my phone call and he seemed to feel quite deeply for me as we talked over a cup of coffee. Oh! how tantalizing it was to have this man's undivided attention. His sympathy made me feel worse and I now felt another pull on my heart as I anticipated the wrench of being parted from him.

Divorce

Ulrika was Sona's steady girlfriend in Sweden—although the admirer who knitted for him was still hoping for more than a brief encounter as he passed through Germany on his way elsewhere. He now had to decide whether to commit himself to working in Sweden. If he wanted to remain there he needed to feel secure in his residency. It looked as if his best bet was to get married.

I tried to give an objective opinion. I didn't like the idea of him marrying again. Marriages of convenience were so rarely straightforward. In our own relationship we had tipped the balance towards friendship and away from marriage. But clinging began with that first kiss and its roots went very, very deep.

If Sona was going to get married, we would first need to get divorced. We thought it might be a good idea to do so anyway. We had not, after all, lived a conventional marriage for some years. Perhaps it would help to clarify our relationship. We would see how much a piece of paper meant.

Three years old

Astride Muffin the mule, with Joanna behind, and Jeremy
(later Lokamitra) bringing up the rear

Sona with the two girls, 1978

Shanti and Sundari during our first visit to Sona in Sweden, 1980

Out walking with Vida (later Kalyanashri), 1973

With Sona in Sweden in 1986,
the year we divorced

Sangharakshita, seated, with (L to R) Do Phillips, me, Shridevi, Padmavati,
and Karunachitta, 1987

With Ashokashri, 1987

My first trip to India,
January 1987

With Lokamitra, his wife Ranjana, and son Ashok, India 1987

The women's ordination
team, summer 1995.
Standing (L to R): Anjali,
me, Dhammadinna,
Sanghadevi, Anoma.
Sitting: Ratnasuri (who
was Beryl), and Samata
(who was Teresa)

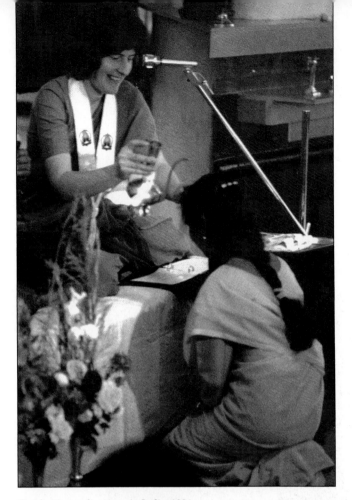

Conducting ordinations in India, 1994

With fellow preceptors Ratnasuri and Sanghadevi at Taraloka, the women's retreat centre, 1989

Sona and Subhuti, 1995

Me and Subhuti, 1995

Sundari, Sona, and Shanti, 1995

My sketch of
Sinhadevi, 1990

Subhuti listening to music, 1989

Crossing the stream, France, 1995

Sinhadevi with cappuccino,
France, 1995

Me with the pink geraniums,
France, 1995

But of course it isn't just a piece of paper: it's the law, it's solicitors, it's other people's feelings and understanding, it's those creeping roots of attachment.

In spite of what I had always tried to convey, for my daughters— Shanti was now twelve and Sundari ten—marriage meant that their parents loved each other and divorce meant that they didn't. I dreaded trying to explain the situation to them. I wished I didn't have to—I couldn't expect them to understand; but it was quite possible they would find out from someone else and that would have been even more disturbing for them. I decided to wait until the proceedings were over, until I had calmed down from the emotional turmoil it was putting me through. I even began to wonder whether in fact I wanted to be married after all. What did I mean by being married? What was it I wanted? Some sort of security, someone to rely on. Was I hankering after that cushionfloor prison again?

I had to trust that the girls would see, unconventional as it might appear, that their Mum and Dad did still love one another.

Ulrika wanted to meet me. She even offered to pay for me and the girls to go over to Sweden. We could have a holiday there with Sona, staying in the house in the woods they were renting for retreats. And maybe I could lead study for a couple of days for the women Mitras; having taken over from Dhammadinna as Convenor of Women Mitras, I could use this rare opportunity to see for myself how they were faring.

I deliberated. I didn't want to feel beholden to Ulrika. But it would be lovely for the girls to have a holiday there, and perhaps it would be a good opportunity to tell them about the divorce.

Heather House was a box-like building, consisting of one main kitchen-living-room and two small bedrooms. The girls argued over who was to have the top bunk. Once a bargain had been struck, they unpacked their bags and arranged their things in the cupboards which lined the wall. In the other room they set up a puppet theatre. They spent hours in there, making puppets and producing plays. Sona made them a swing in the garden and taught Shanti how to throw a javelin.

Sona and I slept, separately, in the living room. It was strange to be sharing a room with him but not a bed. There seemed to be more tension between us than was necessary. I felt very anxious about our forthcoming disclosure to the girls and I didn't really know what I felt about meeting Sona's girlfriend. I wanted to feel closer to Sona and I asked him to share my bed. A little reluctantly he did, but he couldn't enclose me in his arms and reassure me as I'd wanted him to.

It was horrible telling the girls. We were sitting around the break-fast table in the aftermath of a squabble as to who would have the last of the Rice Krispies. We'd put it off long enough. I took another swig of coffee and a deep breath, and asked for everyone's attention. It was obvious that Mum meant business. What on earth was she going to say? A little explosion of giggles from Shanti followed my speech and relieved the tension. Sundari burst into tears. Shanti seemed to realize that her reaction had been inappropriate and she began to sob. Sona and I each took up a bewildered, sobbing little girl into our arms, try-ing to comfort and reassure them. They were so concerned that we should still love each other and that they still had both a mother and a father. Sundari made Sona promise that he wouldn't marry anyone else. The heavy cloud had finally broken and there didn't appear to be too much storm damage. All we could do now was to hope that our example, our sincere efforts to maintain good communication, and our concern for them, would prove that we still loved each other and that we would always be their parents. We would deal with the wed-ding if and when there was one.

The retreat went very well. Sona and I had papered the walls of the hut which was to be used as a shrine-room. We began the retreat by dedicating the freshly-decorated space to the pursuit of En-lightenment. Study was a little slow as we often had to have recourse to the dictionary.

Ulrika was very friendly towards me. She wanted to stay on for a day or two after the retreat, when Sona and the girls came back. I didn't really like the idea, but Sona thought that if that's what she wanted ... after all she'd given up her holiday with him so that I could be there. I tried not to feel obliged to agree, but I couldn't articulate a good enough reason to refuse without looking mean or narrow-minded, so she stayed.

She slept in the puppet theatre. It was strange, knowing that nor-mally they would have been sleeping together.

Ulrika and I went for a walk and talked intensely. She was concerned that her busy job was not helping her to put her under-standing of the Dharma into practice and she was in the midst of a dilemma as to whether to leave it and what to do if she did. Whilst we couldn't avoid mentioning Sona we steered clear of discussing him and our respective relationships with him. We even got on to the sub-ject of whether Ulrika had any desire to have a baby, and I managed to keep my fears to myself. We wandered through the forest and picked mushrooms.

Later we all went out together. We took the little boat to an island and someone instigated a game of hide-and-seek. A game within a game. We weren't ready for it. Trying to be adult we played, but our play brought confused feelings to the surface. I envied the girls as they dashed about, happy, innocent, and honest.

Another Marriage

By the time Sona did get married Sundari was quite amenable to him retracting his promise not to—on condition that he bought her a book!

The day after the wedding Ulrika and I went out for a meal together in London, before attending the launch of Bhante's book, *Ambedkar and Buddhism*. At the launch Sona sat a few rows in front of us and in spite of his jovial manner, he seemed a little nervous as he turned round to greet his two wives.

He wanted me to befriend Ulrika. I was happy to try. When Sona left Sweden in 1988, to live again at Padmaloka, she came to live in Norwich and so we had an opportunity to spend more time together. It wasn't always easy for either of us, but we liked each other well enough to persevere. Perhaps sometimes we tried too hard to keep our jealousy and confused feelings from getting in the way. Sometimes I even believed I didn't feel jealous. But inevitably a festering went on and we were faced with the occasional painful confrontation. And even when we would rather have held one another at arm's length, the context of the Sangha—of striving in spiritual fellowship towards a common goal—forced us, in a sense, to work harder to resolve our negative feelings.

Mostly I felt confident of my friendship with Sona, although it could get a little knocked about in the confusion of our unconventional, undefinable relationships.

Often I experienced a vague, non-specific expectation. I wanted something from him but, unable to say what it was, I couldn't be satisfied. I had to become clearer. I had to consider what I could reasonably expect from him. What did I actually want or need? If I wanted him to be more involved with our daughters, how did I expect that involvement to manifest?

I admitted to myself that I didn't really want to take Sona's marriage seriously—he would always be my husband. Then I reminded myself that I no longer wanted a husband. I wanted to be able to talk openly and honestly with Sona, to speak my mind free from the oversensitivity and suspicion that could taint our communication. I wanted to be free of my own feelings of possessiveness. I began to realize that my non-specific expectation was an old habit, and that all I really wanted was for Sona and me to be friends.

Do what you have to do
Resolutely, with all your heart.
The traveler who hesitates
Only raises dust on the road.

seven

On the Floor at my Feet

The resident men vacated Padmaloka, the men's retreat centre outside Norwich, for ten days leaving Bhante to conduct a seminar for women Order members and Mitras. There was a lot of talk about the differences between men and women and after only a few days we discovered that men eat more bread and women eat more fruit. We talked about some of the advantages and disadvantages of having children, and in particular we tackled a certain rationalization: that if Buddhists had children they would be helping the Sangha to grow. Buddhist parents might well be expected to give their children a wholesome upbringing but it couldn't be assumed that as a result of their doing so, their offspring would necessarily develop faith in the Dharma.

Bhante asked if anyone was able to cut hair. A little tentatively I offered my services. Whilst others were washing up, cleaning, or gardening I went off to Bhante's study where I found him ready for me, with a chair set out in the middle of the room, standing on a few sheets of newspaper.

I hardly dared start cutting. What a precious head I had before me! What if I cut it by mistake? I took a little time to compose myself, studying the longish grey hair before me as though pondering on how to advance on it, and then I just began. Bhante told me about his last visit to his mother, and I relaxed. His sister was having trouble with her teenage daughter and he light-heartedly suggested it was time for her to be married off. I wondered how long it would be before I was thinking in those terms about my own daughters.

When my job was done I stood back to admire my work. Bhante glanced at himself in a mirror. Then, before I realized what was happening, he was down on his hands and knees picking up the newspaper from the floor. I stood looking down foolishly at my teacher, the man I should be looking up to. He was in my place on the floor, on his hands and knees at my feet.

Working Together

For many years the transcribing of Bhante's spoken words remained an important activity for me. It was something I could easily do whilst being very much tied to the home. I had given up the idea of a community. I wasn't committed to classes at the Centre, apart from a morning study group, because I didn't want to spend more than one or two nights in a week away from my children. There were plenty of women around but we had no community or team-based Right Livelihood business. We lacked a more intensive situation which could bring us together, give us an opportunity to work together, offer us more of a challenge, and perhaps help some to move nearer to ordination. Many of us were mothers but we no longer talked of schools and family communities. We still had occasional outings and holidays together, and we put on special events for the children at the Centre on festival days. However, these were not long-term projects, and our enthusiasm for doing things with the children waned as they grew older and less amenable to our plans. We now needed special events for ourselves, events which didn't include the children.

When Subhuti saw that I wanted a project, he asked me to organize advance subscriptions for the publication of his first book, *Buddhism for Today*. When the book was printed, I took on responsibility for its distribution within the movement. I was glad to be able to do this, but I was still working very much on my own. Sometimes I would invite a friend round to help me address envelopes. More often than not the work would take longer than when I did it alone because no one was content to get on without having a good old chat as well. I began to realize that there was more to working together than met the eye.

Then Subhuti turned up with the very thing. He had taken over the editing of the magazine *Mitrata*, and he needed help. First of all someone was needed to type the contents of each issue. Then the copy needed to be prepared and sent off to the printers. By this time, 1983, I had been women's Mitra Convenor in Norwich for six years, and had got to know the women Mitras. Between us, we had a number of skills—and spare time. Having realized the potential amongst the women in Norwich, Subhuti suggested another way we could help. The magazine consisted of a lecture by Bhante followed by extracts from his seminars further illustrating the subject of each issue. To begin with, Subhuti had had to rely on his own memory. Now he suggested that we could search through the transcribed seminars for suitable extracts ourselves. It was ideal work for those of us who were mothers. We would mostly be working at home, but we would be working in connection with others, and through our work we would be studying the Dharma and helping to communicate it more widely.

Vida, who had finally left her husband and seen the light of the Dharma, was a keen transcriber. Sue, with her typing skills, was ready to get down to work. Beryl too, with whom Sue and the typewriter lived, wanted to help. Together we formed the *Mitrata* Production Team.

As we got going with our work other women, mostly mothers, began to join us. Between us we were able to search through most of Bhante's transcribed seminars. We acquired a computer and improved the quality, design, and layout of our publication. We found a local printer and took over responsibility for printing and distribution. Eventually I became the managing editor and we took over the production of *Mitrata* from start to finish.

We acquired a more substantial office and, with Sue prepared to work full-time, we took on the production of other one-off publications. We were now no longer simply the *Mitrata* Production Team. We turned ourselves into a charity and called it Lion's Roar.

My friendship with Vida had moved firmly on to a different footing. Although our children, shopping, and washing were still very much a part of our lives, we had in *Mitrata*, a spiritually stimulating project to bring us together. However, even though we now had a more meaningful basis from which to relate, we didn't always see eye to eye. Vida had begun to take on some sub-editing from me and, both amateurs at the work, we argued as to where a comma should go!

I especially enjoyed working with Sue. It seemed as though she was always in the office. I would frequently take my work round there to be in her company rather than on my own. I admired her dedication to her work and the orderliness with which she kept the office. She watched over me as I discovered the delights of 'pasting-up'. We drank tea together and tried not to spend too much time chatting about her intriguing love life. We both took a particular pride in each issue of *Mitrata*. After meticulously scouring the prepared copy for mistakes and then double-checking our instructions to the printers for any ambiguity, together we would hand over our precious charge.

Slowly, as we worked on Mitrata, it worked on us. We had a concrete project, so much bigger than ourselves and our children, with which we could engage. I personally felt that through Lion's Roar my energies were more satisfyingly engaged in working for the Dharma than they had ever been before and my communication was much less likely, therefore, to succumb to the details and demands of family life.

No Reason to Resign

I often experienced frustration in my work as Convenor of women Mitras. I was now involved with the spiritual welfare not just of the women Mitras who lived in Norwich, but of women in many countries throughout the world. They could write to me, they could visit me, but I couldn't travel around as my predecessor, Dhammadinna, had done, and I couldn't stop myself from thinking that I was therefore not able to do the job as it should ideally be done. Sometimes I wondered whether I should resign.

I talked with Bhante about my frustrations. He wouldn't let me dwell on them. When I said I lacked the freedom to do my job properly he asked me to consider what being free really meant. He saw no reason for me to resign, and simply encouraged me to deepen my friendships with the other Mitra Convenors.

In my heart of hearts I knew he was right. And in any case there was no one else willing and able to do the job. I knew I could still be more creative in the way I worked. My time and energy were naturally limited, but freedom was not to be found in waiting for the end of dirty nappies, the start of school, the passing by of each two-year phase of motherhood. There were more fundamental restrictions than these to be dealt with. It was the chains of Greed, Hatred, and Ignorance that I had to sever. I had to become like wrathful Vajrapani who, in a fury of flames, breaks through from the mundane to the transcendental. And friendship, it appeared, should be my tool.

Mission Joyfully Accomplished

Not long after my brother had been ordained as Lokamitra, he launched a fund-raising appeal which culminated in the acquisition of an old fire station in East London—a building ideal for conversion into the new London Buddhist Centre. His next project was to prove even more demanding and long-term. Whilst visiting India on a yoga course he met with a very warm reception as a disciple of Sangharakshita. He came to the conclusion that the FWBO was badly needed in India and in 1978 he decided to move there in order to develop Dharma activities.

Lokamitra eventually got married and in December 1985 he became a father. My mother then began to plan a trip to India to visit him and his new family. I asked her if she would like company and she agreed to take me with her.

I was keen to go, both to see Lokamitra at home in India and to experience the manifestation of our movement there. I always read the reports of Order members working in India with great interest and admiration, and from the numerous slide shows I'd seen I felt I had some idea of what it would be like. However, others who had been already warned me that one could never be prepared.

I was getting extremely excited about going. I'd even asked Bhante whether there was anything particular he would like me to do whilst I was there. And then my mother found that she couldn't go that year after all. I was so disappointed. I had been going to accompany her and now my trip was cancelled. But did it have to be? Someone suggested that I should go anyway. I could fund-raise for the airfare.

And so with renewed vigour I set about finding customers for the meditation cushions that my friend Padmavati and I were making. After many an hour on my knees, cutting out the green cotton drill, and then whirring away on my sewing machine, I had raised half my fare. The rest I would borrow and pay back with the proceeds of a slide show on my return.

Now that I was definitely going, Bhante did have something he wanted me to do. He wanted me to take Ratnasuri (my talkative friend Beryl, now ordained) with me and, together with Padmasuri who was already there, to conduct, on his behalf, the ordinations of two Indian women. Fortunately we were talking on the phone and so he didn't see the look of incredulity on my face. I tried to swallow my astonishment and said I would contact Ratnasuri right away. Of course I was prepared to do what he'd asked, but my goodness, how could I ordain someone? In spite of the fact that as Convenor of Women Mitras I had been helping to oversee the ordination process for women, and although I had been ordained myself for nearly twelve years, I had never imagined that I might one day be so directly concerned with one of Bhante's most crucial responsibilities.

To conduct an ordination meant, in essence, to witness another person's Going for Refuge; to witness their declaration of commitment to the only real refuges, the Three Jewels of the Buddha, the Dharma, and the Sangha. It meant acting as a preceptor, witnessing an undertaking to live according to the Ten Precepts: an undertaking to act skilfully with body, speech, and mind, aspiring to emulate, and ultimately to become, an Enlightened being. It meant witnessing and blessing such a crucial turning point in someone's life.

Several years previously Bhante had asked the Order to consider who might conduct ordinations in the future. I was struck at the time to realize that I simply couldn't imagine anyone else conducting ordinations, let alone envisage a time when that would be necessary —when Bhante was no longer with us. I'm afraid I didn't even try to contemplate further. Then, a couple of years later, Bhante asked three Dharmacharis to conduct the men's ordinations in India. Perhaps if there were some women ready to be ordained, they would ordain them too. But no, it transpired that in sharing his responsibility for conferring ordination, Bhante had decided that it would be Dharmacharinis who would ordain women. After all, with our emphasis on single-sex activities it was Dharmacharinis who, on the whole, knew the women best and who were most involved in the consideration and encouragement of their requests for ordination.

Shortly before my departure I visited Bhante. He explained that for women to be ordaining women was to make history. I began to feel even more nervous than I had been. Many women outside the FWBO, he said, were frustrated in their attempts to devote themselves to the spiritual life. The problem was in thinking that their only way ahead was to become *bhikkhunis*. But the *bhikkhuni* ordination had been kept alive only in China and Korea, and even there the traditional requirements were extremely difficult to meet. Furthermore, the ordination was complete only after it had been accepted by a chapter of *bhikkhus*, the leading of a spiritual life, according to tradition, therefore seemed to depend finally on men. Within the FWBO, he said, such restrictions did not apply.

On parting Bhante left me with a little advice. Something to bear in mind during the ordination ceremony, I presumed. No, it seemed he was more concerned about my physical well-being. He warned me to drink boiled water and not to rely only on flip-flops. The ground around the retreat centre at Bhaja was quite rough and thorny, so I would need a pair of good, strong shoes.

The launch of Bhante's book *Ambedkar and Buddhism* (which I attended with Ulrika and Sona) provided me with a very timely send-off. On my flight I finished the remarkable story of Dr Ambedkar and his long road to conversion. Having been born into the most under-privileged and downtrodden of backgrounds, he became India's first Law Minister and chief architect of her constitution. His career culminated in his conversion to Buddhism, taking with him half a million others who like himself had formerly been considered, within the Hindu caste system, 'Untouchable'.

Within twenty minutes of stepping off the plane I was standing in the glaring sun accosted by porters reaching out to take my bags. I saw Lokamitra and felt, in a way, at home. I hadn't seen him for some years. He was eager for news of England and with little to offer him I immediately felt inadequate. We took a taxi to the station and I realized I felt somewhat stunned. I gave up trying to search my mind for any snippet of information that might be of interest and gazed, open-mouthed, at my surroundings. It was nearly evening but the sun was still beating down. The tarmac road we were driving down was under construction. It was being constructed by hand. Men, women, and children were crushing stones, boiling up black tar, wandering to and fro amidst the traffic, squatting at the side of the road, living their lives in the dust, filth, and fumes.

Having just missed a train up to Poona we took a 'first-class' taxi instead. Squashed in the back with Lokamitra and one of the other three passengers, I clung on to the seat in front. We raced along, swerving through the crazy traffic, sometimes to avoid the lorries that hurtled towards us in the dark with no lights. Our driver appeared to be determined to get us to Poona in record time—dead or alive! I simply couldn't believe the risks that he took as we drove uphill round hairpin bends with a sheer drop to our left. Tired, disorientated, and rigid with tension, I hoped I wasn't meant to die just then.

Arriving at Poona, a short rickshaw ride took us to our destination. It seemed that I was finally on firm ground. I could at last relax. I knew that Lokamitra didn't approve of giving Westerners a gentle introduction to India. I discovered, however, that my own introduction had been somewhat rough, even by his standards, as he actually apologized to me for it.

I met Ranjana, my sister-in-law, and Ashok, my year-old nephew, for the first time. I had last seen Lokamitra when he was still single. We had spent a few days away with my mother and my two daughters. It had been rather a strain all round. Now I was seeing my older brother in the midst of his young family whilst I was enjoying a respite from my maternal responsibilities. Even here in India my family and spiritual life were intertwined. I handed round the presents I'd brought over with me, the most successful by far being the Christmas cake.

We sat on the kitchen floor to eat and I managed quite well with my fingers, sitting on my left hand in order to observe the custom of not eating with it. Padmasuri appeared, fresh from her evening's 'programme'—a Dharma talk, given in the open air, under floodlights, to hundreds of eager listeners. She was pleased to see me and so very happy that now two Indian women would shortly be ordained.

Soon I was lying under a mosquito net letting the vivid impressions soak in and trying to sleep through the unfamiliar sounds around me.

The next day Padmasuri took me to get measured up for a sari blouse. I pleaded for it not to be too tight. But even loose, I later discovered, was tight.

Then Ratnasuri arrived. And so we were now the ordination team. Padmasuri unobtrusively took us in hand. In her competent, kind, and sensitive manner she taught us to watch where we put our feet, how to sit down and stand up in a sari with decency and poise, and how, when invited for a meal in someone's home, to avoid eating too much without being rude.

For several years Padmasuri had lived in India for six months of each year, first working within the social welfare project our movement had started there, but then devoting herself to Dharma activities and working more closely with women who wanted to be ordained.

One afternoon two fifteen-year-old girls came to visit us. A little shy of Ratnasuri and myself, they were delightfully at ease with Padmasuri, and with both obvious respect and playful familiarity they begged her to tell them the story of why the Three Jewels were the colours they were. Without hesitation Padmasuri obliged and we all listened, enthralled, to her simple yet deeply moving tale of the blue sky, the brilliant sun, and a compassionate heart.

We took the train out to the retreat centre at Bhaja and spent a few days preparing ourselves before the fifteen or so Mitras arrived. We planned the programme for the retreat and, most importantly, we learned our lines. Although most of the ordination ceremony was familiar to us we would be required to speak a little Hindi, especially Ratnasuri, who was to conduct the public ceremony. One afternoon we walked across the parched fields, through the dusty village and up to the ancient Buddhist caves. We sat ourselves down in the two-thousand-year-old stupa hall and practised our chanting of the blessings.

Mrs Kharat and Mrs Labhane arrived on retreat looking radiant. After several years of wanting to take this step they were finally going to be ordained into the Western Buddhist Order (or Trailokya Bauddha Mahasangha as it is known in India). They were both a few years older than me. Mrs Kharat had three children and Mrs Labhane had five. I heard snippets of the lives of these two women: of the slum conditions that Mrs Kharat had been living in; of the dedicated work of Mrs Labhane which had once ended in a spell in prison. I felt humbled by their devotion to Dr Ambedkar, and to Bhante, who had taken up the great leader's work and made possible a context in which their commitment as Buddhists would be encouraged and strengthened.

All the retreatants had come from the ex-Untouchable community. They were mostly mothers and grandmothers, although there were several unmarried girls too. One woman was illiterate, another was a schoolteacher.

In my own life I had struggled, but what were my struggles compared to the ones these women had gone through? I wanted to do what I could for them. As we sat outside one afternoon during one of our delightful tea breaks, entwined in each other's arms and chatting intimately, I was called upon to sing. Despite being prepared to overcome my embarrassment, I couldn't oblige. After their moving Buddhist devotional songs I simply couldn't think of anything remotely appropriate. In the end someone suggested a Beatles' song, 'Yellow Submarine', and we all joined in.

I was determined that my sense of inadequacy shouldn't interfere with the joy, the solemnity, the magic, of the forthcoming ceremonies. I must forget about myself and my own worries and concentrate on the tremendous step that these two women were about to take, a step that would not only transform them but also help to change the lives of so many more to come. It was enough, I reflected, that Bhante had confidence in me to act on his behalf.

A special shrine was prepared for the private ceremonies—a tent of blue flowing saris enclosing a white shrine on which sat a delicate golden Buddha. Beneath him was a photograph of Bhante. From the main shrine-room, rows of night lights directed the way to the spot where the two women would formally commit themselves to the Three Jewels. As I led Mrs Labhane through the ceremony and pronounced her new name, Jnanasuri, I felt my own commitment, my own Going for Refuge, resounding with hers, and I experienced once again the extraordinary impact of my own ordination. We had known each other only a few days and, through my witnessing what was probably the most important step she would ever take, we had formed a bond that would last the rest of our lives.

Hundreds of people turned up for the public ceremony, which was held outside under a canopy. When it was over we sent a telegram to Bhante saying, 'Mission joyfully accomplished'. Then we spent a delightful few days getting to know our new sisters in the Dharma, leading them through their new meditation practices and initiating them into the ways of the Order. When the time came to leave, our partings were wet with tears. Both Ratnasuri and I hoped we would be back again, but we had no idea when that might be.

This was the second time I'd been away from my home and daughters for a month. My solitary retreat had had a strong effect on me but the effect of this experience, I sensed, would be even more marked. I felt definitely changed by it, though I couldn't describe how. I'd seen so much more of life, raw life. I'd met with such friendliness and positivity. I'd encountered a more tangible appreciation of the Buddha, and more heartfelt devotion and faith than I'd ever met with before. I'd been shocked, fascinated, and horrified by the conditions in which so many people were living: the poverty, suffering, filth, and degradation. At times I longed to be back at home. And yet, when I boarded my plane at Bombay, I felt as though I was literally wrenching myself away. India, the land of the Buddha, and her vibrant inhabitants, had had their effect upon me.

As I flew back to England, I recalled the retreat at Bhaja and jotted down notes for an editorial for *Mitrata*. For weeks I remained in India in my dreams.

Whilst I had been away there had been a lot of snow—so much, in fact, that the girls hadn't been able to go to school for a week. Sona had looked after them well, but they'd missed me and were very glad to have me back.

The Weight of Responsibility

Three years after my first trip to India, I received another significant and startling phone call from Bhante. When I returned home from an Order weekend, my daughters told me that he had phoned. I couldn't imagine why. A few days later he called again. What were my plans for the summer, he asked. Suddenly the penny dropped: Bhante was asking me if I could attend the ordination retreat, if I could form an ordination team with Ratnasuri and Sanghadevi.... My grip on the telephone grew tighter and tighter as I tried to sound matter-of-fact. I had previously convinced myself that this wouldn't happen—probably because I felt an enormous reluctance to take on such a responsibility—and so I was taken by surprise. How could I say, 'Bhante, I don't feel up to it'? Helping him to share and pass on this responsibility was of vital importance both to him and to the future of the Order. I felt honoured that he'd asked me. I couldn't but respond. I felt strangely confident, affected by his confidence in me, and at the same time terrified of the implications of saying yes. I put the phone down and burnt the meal I was cooking.

The ordinations could not be seen as an isolated event this time: we would have to be prepared to be preceptors and gradually to bear the responsibility for ordaining women into the Western Buddhist Order. And there would be no excitement of a trip to a foreign land.

Three years previously I had experienced the great joy and profundity of ordaining someone. Why, I wondered, did I now feel such resistance? Bhante had spoken of the responsibility as being an expression of our own commitment. Did I feel that my commitment was not strong enough to be so expressed?

Before the ordinations I went away on solitary retreat. I had hoped to prepare myself, to shed the resistance I felt and reflect on the implications of what we were doing. I returned home to go straight to Taraloka, the women's retreat centre, which had been running retreats for some time after years of planning, fund-raising, and building work by women Order members, Mitras, and Friends. In the midst of an Order gathering, I acknowledged that my reflections had simply shown me that I was suffering, quite severely, from self-doubt. As the ordination retreat approached, I determined that my resistance to further responsibility and my self-doubt would not deny me my part in it. I tried to fathom just exactly what I was doing in witnessing another's Going for Refuge, and what my duties would be towards someone I had ordained. Perhaps, I thought, I had been expecting too much of myself.

I wanted to do lots of meditation, in preparation, but my circumstances at home wouldn't permit that. Shanti and Sundari, now sixteen and fourteen, had arrived home from their holiday in France and they were full of endless stories. Instead of trying to meditate more, I could practise patience; and I could be more wholehearted about whatever I was doing—cooking, washing the dishes, listening. I acknowledged that I wouldn't achieve perfection overnight but I could make an effort to develop and maintain a positive state of mind.

I wanted to see the girls off on their first day back at school before leaving them to go on retreat. I therefore missed the pre-retreat meeting when the Order team met to tune in together and discuss final details. Once again I was in the position of feeling on the edge of things, not quite able to be fully involved. At times I caught myself wondering why I wasn't at home with my children, leading an ordinary sort of life.

One by one, six women ventured into the dark and, one by one, they returned to the shrine-room, transformed. On the nights when I conducted the ordinations of Silaprabha and Jayadevi, I was positively glowing. 'What a wonderful thing to do!' I kept remarking to myself.

forced

Once the retreat was over, my self-doubt built up again and during the following months I subjected myself to a pretty tough examination. If I were to witness the Going for Refuge of others, I reflected, I simply must be sincerely going for Refuge myself. The Buddha, Dharma, and Sangha should be firmly established at the centre of my mandala. I questioned whether they were. Even after fourteen years as an Order member, were they truly the three most precious Jewels in my life? Where did they really stand? How close to the centre would I put my immediate Sangha, my women friends? How important were they to me? Should they be more important to me than my daughters? And if I was honest wouldn't I say that I regarded my ex-husband and my lover as my closest friends?

It was a very painful time. I had, I thought, been working so hard to loosen, or at least not to strengthen, my romantic and familial attachments. I thought I appreciated the vital importance of *kalyana mitrata* —the whole of the spiritual life. Why then had I not accomplished more through my efforts to develop friendships with women? Could the men in my life really be holding me back? How could I ask someone to repeat after me the Three Refuges and the Ten Precepts when I knew that I wasn't always living in accordance with them?

My reflections fed my doubt and I undermined myself further. I couldn't see at the time that they were the basis from which to move on. I was trying to understand why I didn't consider myself worthy of being a preceptor. Could it simply be understandable resistance—the gravitational pull—to a spiritual challenge, or was there really something wrong with me?

A Timely Blow

On retreat at Taraloka, I gave a talk entitled 'Leaving Mother, Father, Husband, and Children Too'. Giving the talk served to remind me of the efforts I had made to Go Forth. After months of questioning, I was feeling a little more sure of myself, unaware of the blow that was to come.

At the end of the retreat, a friend invited me for a walk. We set off up the track. Our relations had been a bit constrained of late. We had been friends at a distance for a number of years; then eventually Ashokashri moved up to Norwich and our friendship had a chance to blossom. I had thought this might at last be an opportunity for friendship to take a more substantial place in my life. But I was too much in need; I was clumsy and I found that I'd hoped for more than was possible.

Now it seemed our walk had a purpose to it and contrary to my initial, hopeful expectations, it was not a pleasant one. Ashokashri began by saying that she wasn't finding it easy trying to say what she had on her mind. In the uncomfortable silence that followed, I thought to myself, 'Well I'm obviously not going to find it easy to listen to, so perhaps you shouldn't bother!' She wanted to give me some feedback. Already I was in no mood to receive any, but as feedback is supposed to be helpful, I braced myself. She told me that my doubting of myself had encouraged a questioning, a doubting of me, in her mind. I was devastated. I suddenly realized how much I needed her to have confidence in me. It was one thing to doubt myself, but if one of my closest friends was beginning to doubt me what chance did I have of recovering my confidence? We returned down the track in heavy silence. I was so angry I could have exploded, but no word would reach my lips.

That dreadful feedback proved to be just what I needed. The point went sharply home and, when the pain had subsided, I took a good look at my wound. The self-doubt I had been experiencing was bad enough. Now through my indulgence it had spread. I hadn't seen to what extent it could work against me. It had affected someone else, someone I had relied on to believe in me. I was spurred on to acknowledge my faith in the Three Jewels and to realize my own self-confidence. I had been suffering from doubt, one of the Three Fetters that prevent us from making irreversible progress on the path to Enlightenment, but that didn't mean I wasn't sincerely going for Refuge. My heart, I decided, was most definitely in the right place.

My expectations of myself *had* been too high. I had thought that in order to be worthy of conferring ordination I needed to be almost perfect—a Stream Entrant, one who had broken the Three Fetters. I knew now that that was not the case. I had been waiting for something to happen that would make me worthy of being a preceptor. But nothing was going to happen. All I had to do was to take my attention away from my own unworthiness and place it on what I was actually doing and on the importance of that action for Bhante and the growth of the Order. Whether I was wonderfully worthy or not, I had taken on the responsibility. I wanted to do what I was doing as well as I was able. I just needed to get on with it, and in that way I would eventually break through my resistance and self-doubt.

I had been feeling pulled in two apparently opposing directions. I felt frustrated, as I so often did, by my conditions—manifesting in the form of my two daughters. My priority as a preceptor was surely to be involved as much as I possibly could be with the ordination process for women and all that that entailed: going on retreat at Taraloka, working with the rest of the team, and with women preparing for ordination. If I did this, it would mean leaving my daughters as much as I possibly could. But how would I decide what was possible? And what was possible might not necessarily be wise. My daughters would be with me at home for another few years. I had to work from that basis—from being with them as much as was necessary, rather than from trying to get away from them as much as was possible. The question for me was no longer, was I up to it, but rather, how I could do what I was doing more effectively, taking into account my circumstances? If I was clear about my situation I could commit myself, and by committing myself I could be more effective. It was as simple as that. I didn't need to have left home absolutely; I didn't need to be a Stream Entrant; I just needed to be making an effort in the right direction.

A Friend on my Doorstep

Over the years Subhuti had encouraged me to make more of my friendships with women. I knew it made sense. I knew that I shouldn't rely so much on him for intimacy. But I seemed to have so little opportunity to take my friendships further. At least with him we both had a vested interest in making time for one another.

From time to time seemingly contradictory thoughts would play on my mind. What was the point of continued exertion when it was doubtful that my efforts would bear fruit? Would anyone have the time for me anyway? My emotions didn't seem to accord with my understanding—could love be blinding me? I had tried to take on board the idea that true *kalyana mitrata* was not to be found within a sexual relationship—craving and attachment, which invariably accompany sex, having no place in the self-transcending love of *kalyana mitrata*. I thought I ought to feel that I was in some way held back by my sexual involvement with Subhuti. In fact I felt I benefited enormously from my relationship with him. Of course I experienced a certain amount of longing at times, even pain and confusion, but it was a small price to pay. I couldn't imagine any of my friendships with women, no matter how much I cultivated them, becoming more important to me than my relationship with Subhuti.

I saw before me a painting of Tobias and the Angel. It was a beautiful example of spiritual love: one friend gently leading another on, away from the pain and restriction of worldly life, and towards the bliss and freedom of the heavenly realm. It was a depiction of *brahmacharya,* the divine life, in which sexual desire is transcended through the practice of chastity and the cultivation of clear, refined, and uplifted awareness; a life traditionally considered to be the most conducive to the attainment of the Buddhist goal of Enlightenment.

If I was concerned to develop *kalyana mitrata* it seemed I must do so outside the context of a sexual relationship. And if *kalyana mitrata* was really so special—the whole of the spiritual life, according to the Buddha—then such friendships would be more important to me than one that involved sex. The trouble was I didn't really want any other relationship to be more important to me. I also didn't really believe that there was no element of *kalyana mitrata* in my relationship with Subhuti. I was convinced that my association with him had contributed to my growth as an individual. I had benefited not only from emotional and physical intimacy, but also from his intellectual stimulation, his interest in my life and work, his encouragement, his generosity, his understanding, and his inspiring example. He had helped me to discard the view I cherished of myself as being inadequate, inarticulate, and lacking in confidence, and he had inspired me to fan the flames of faith. He had helped me to find ways of expressing myself more effectively, to find my voice and to use it. Despite the precariousness of a sexual relationship and the knowledge that I couldn't rely on Subhuti as a lover, I found that there were many other ways in which he was to be relied on. It was hard not to think of him as a spiritual friend.

In my heart of hearts I was confused. I was aware of some sort of holding back. I knew that my experience of *kalyana mitrata* was still very limited and that I myself felt limited through my lack of close, non-sexual, friendship.

I came home from retreat determined to find a friend. It would still be some time before I could live in a community but surely I could find a friend on my doorstep, someone with whom I could talk every day, someone who had my best interests at heart and I hers, someone with whom I could share my joys and my sorrows, my hopes and my fears, my life.

I think I took Kalyanashri (my old friend Vida) rather by surprise when I told her I wanted to see more of her. How about every day? I was even prepared to walk up the hill to her house. But once again I was too clumsy. I was feeling almost desperate, as though if I didn't force myself I would passively let opportunities go by and be left

escating as fact but not formally acknowledged as such

frustrated. I knew that it wouldn't be easy with Kalyanashri, but surely as such old friends we had a good basis from which to go deeper.

We went for a walk in the woods. Feeling that I must unburden myself, I told her I had felt hurt by something she had said to me. The lid was off. At last we had begun to acknowledge a trail of resentments about one another. We needed time to cool off before we could hope to try and listen to each other further. So we didn't meet for a week or so and then it was a long time before we really wanted to spend more time together.

Do was a good friend but our meetings were sporadic. She had been experiencing some reaction to the movement and so, for a while, there were some no-go areas with her. Really my friend should be a Dharmacharini—someone with whom I could discuss absolutely anything. And maybe, I began to think, it needed to be someone who was not a mother. I had become a little sceptical as to how far friendships between mothers could go. Communication so easily revolved around our children and related domestic issues. In theory we wanted to be more supportive to one another, more actively involved in one another's lives, but in practice we had our hands full with our own. Many of us were trying to be, at least for some of the time, both father and mother to our children. We needed support. Sometimes we just wished for a childless fairy to come and romp around with our children or help us to fix the leaking tap. A friend without children wouldn't need a baby-sitter if she wanted to visit.

Really I wanted someone who was always interested in me, who always had time for me, with whom I could say almost anything that was on my mind. I had to admit that what I wanted was unreasonable and I acknowledged that, if I wanted a friend, the only way to find one was to be one.

A Dream Come True

I first met Catherine when she came to visit me at my home in Norwich in January 1990. She was on her way to spend two months on solitary retreat in the Norfolk countryside. She had been having a difficult time. She wanted to be ordained, but it seemed that her communication with Order members in London was riddled with misunderstandings. She told me that she had been likened to a bull in a china shop. I told her what Bhante had said to someone in a similar position: 'There shouldn't be so many china shops!'

I found Catherine refreshingly direct, sincere, and intelligent. Although she was obviously very upset by recent events, she could, as she related it all to me, see the funny side. Soon her troubles were forgotten and, beneath the gaze of Botticelli angels and over another cup of tea, we chatted on until it was time for her to catch her bus. She asked if she could visit me on her way back from her solitary retreat and I was very pleased for her to do so.

Catherine returned, bringing a touch of Irish magic with her. We had both thoroughly enjoyed our first encounter. She had, it seemed, benefited from my willingness to listen at a time when she had felt misunderstood, and I had felt nourished by her stimulating and genuinely friendly company. Now she told me of her dreams and the study she had been doing. I mentioned that I had recently done a little drawing and she insisted that I show her my work. I was encouraged by her sensitive and appreciative comments.

From then on Catherine took whatever opportunity she could to visit me, and several months later we spent two weeks together on the same retreat. We got to know each other a bit more and in the silent periods whilst she sat reading I drew her portrait.

She was not happy in London and decided to move to Cambridge, which suited me as it meant we could meet up much more easily. Sinhadevi was very partial to hanging out in choice cafés and she very soon discovered Henry's. Whenever I went to Cambridge we would meet there, at a table overlooking the river, and talk for hours over our cappuccino and Danish pastries.

When Catherine's ordination request was finally agreed, I was to be her private preceptor. We had grown very fond of one another and it was a most fitting token of our friendship for me to be witnessing the formal expression of her effective Going for Refuge. I felt I knew her well enough to choose her name. Over the previous few years, whilst Bhante had not conducted the ordinations, he had still chosen the names. This year Ratnasuri, Sanghadevi, and I decided to think them up ourselves and then see if they met with his approval. I was a little dismayed when, only a few days before the ordination ceremony, Catherine announced that she would like Bhante to choose her name. Rather reluctantly I told him of her request. He asked what name I had come up with and said he would consider it. When I phoned him back a couple of days later, he said he couldn't think of a more appropriate name than the one I had chosen.

And so Catherine became Sinhadevi—the Lion Goddess. Her name had a very particular association with my own. There is a Mahayana sutra called *The Lion's Roar of Queen Srimala*. The lion's roar is a declaration of truth and the term is often used to describe the speech of the

Buddha. Sinhadevi was always concerned to get to the truth of a matter, sometimes like a dog worrying a bone, and she was never afraid, no matter how alone she might be, to proclaim it. As a child she had been called Mrs Mouse. Even now her shyness was apparent, but her dedication to the truth wouldn't let it get the better of her. I found her a most appropriate companion as she often managed to stimulate and encourage me to express my own latent roar.

It was Sinhadevi who first spoke of wanting to make more of our friendship. I had thought I was quite content with the way things were. I felt a little resistant, recalling my efforts in the past. What did she mean? Why did we have to get so self-conscious about it? Deep down I was aware that I was holding back. It was as if the back door had been left open; if I felt I'd had enough I could leave. But she was asking me to close that door and make a further commitment to our friendship—to seal it for better or for worse, like marriage, only there could be no divorce. I would have to make my friendship with her a priority in my life. It would be my duty, and a duty not taken on wholeheartedly could become a chore.

Here was a friend suggesting I make my dream come true and I was feeling a little sceptical—or was I just being realistic? We had the ideal beginnings. What was I afraid of? Could it be that I was afraid I would no longer have a need or an excuse to rely so much on my lover? Was I unwilling for her to claim a place in my life as important as, or even more important than, the one I gave to him? Was I afraid that she would expect more of me than I could give? Was I afraid that I would hope for too much from her? Or was I afraid that she would discover what a boring, shallow person I really was?

Faced with such an opportunity my resistance to further change came into play. But Sinhadevi was able gently to prod my depths and to draw out the best in me. We seemed to complement one another very well. We would naturally rejoice in each other's merits and in our good fortune at having become friends. When I dared to show her some of my writing, her response of sincere, enthusiastic appreciation meant a great deal to me and gave me further confidence to continue. She was also a woman inspired by *brahmacharya* and although she herself was in the early stages of a new love affair whilst I was seriously considering the celibate life, she applauded my uneven steps towards the goal and heard with compassion my confession of each slip backwards.

We looked into the future wondering what it would bring for each of us. She had been visiting FWBO centres in America, leading retreats and generally helping out, and was considering moving there—why didn't I go too? I was about to commit myself to regular visits to India

—why didn't she join me? Perhaps we could work together in some way. Ever since I'd stopped working on *Mitrata* some years before I had missed the pleasures and demands of a close working relationship. She was always interested in my work and I wondered how she could help me. She was enthusiastically willing to do whatever she could. She would even be willing to move, for my sake, to the dull cultural backwater that she considered Norwich to be.

In a matter of weeks she found a flat just five minutes walk away from me. We met up every day, either at her place, my place, or one of Norwich's cafés—none of which, unfortunately, compared with Henry's. We worked together, played together, let off steam together, confessed to one another, challenged one another, cared for one another, misunderstood one another, upset one another, got to know one another more deeply, and desired the very best for each other.

When I went to India again in December 1992, Sinhadevi came too. She proved to be an excellent companion. In spite of her professed terror, especially when crossing roads, she was much more adventurous than I was and managed the food and heat better than I could. I was impressed by her boldness, her resourcefulness, her readiness to engage, and her delightful gullibility. On retreat she would massage my tense shoulders and encourage me on when I showed signs of getting overwhelmed. We would compare our sufferings—hard mattresses and room-mates who snored; and our fantasies—soft mattresses and cream cakes.

My dream had come true and there was, happily, no escaping it.

Happiness or sorrow—
Whatever befalls you,
Walk on
Untouched, unattached.

eight

I Wanted to Find my Voice

On the way up to Taraloka Vajragita told me about the book she was reading: *To the Is-Land*. The train was making such a noise it was hard to catch what she said. What the author had been through sounded a bit gruesome.

Hoping for good weather we had decided to share a tent and when we were tucked up in our sleeping bags one night, I asked Vajragita to read to me from her book. As she read the evocative descriptions of train journeys, people and places, and moving house, I could almost hear the rattling of the railway in the background repeating the rhythmical names of the passing stations, just as the author had done. On returning home I bought the book—the early years in the autobiography of Janet Frame—and the two accompanying volumes.

For the last couple of years I had been wrestling with a new responsibility—being a preceptor. I had created more space in my life in order to encourage the process of adjustment and do whatever was required of me—and indeed, to consider just what was required of me. I had recently turned forty, I had been ordained for sixteen years, and my time as a dedicated mother was coming to an end. In spite of my simplified life-style I felt little enthusiasm for much of what I was doing and experienced a strong sense of dissatisfaction. I felt in need of some sort of change or break.

I read *To the Is-Land* and *An Angel at my Table*. Janet Frame was determined to be a poet and a writer. Her writing, her aspiration, and her honesty immediately appealed to me. She was extremely shy, but through her determination she overcame the obstacles in her way, including her own resistance. I was moved by her honesty in relating how she did as others wanted her to. I was amused by her behaviour, until it led to disastrous results. She spoke of New Zealanders 'speaking for themselves', finding their own voice. Something within me was stirred, moved, excited; a chord had been struck and I wanted it to resonate.

[handwritten margin notes: "applied, field or domain of activity" and "a intate of existence between death + rebirth"]

Within a week I knew what I wanted to do. I would take a break for three months. Ideally I would have gone to a Greek island—somewhere far away, surrounded by sea, and graced by the sun—but as I couldn't do that I planned to turn my bedroom into an island. I would make it known that I was unavailable—to everyone except my daughters and one or two friends. Then, alone and undisturbed, I wanted to find my voice. Inspired by Janet Frame I had decided that writing would be my medium.

I was in the midst of great change, hovering in a *bardo*, an in-between state, a watershed in my life. My *raison d'être* in one realm was ceasing to be, but in another it was taking on a more definite shape. I had entered another episode in the story of my leaving home and Going Forth. Perhaps I could begin to write up that story.

On 16 September 1991 my island retreat officially began. I still hadn't decided what I would do with my mail. I thought I would probably let it pile up and then glance at it once a week so that I could deal with anything urgent. As I picked up the few letters that had already arrived, I remembered one that I was expecting over the next few months. I found that it was already in my hand—from the hospital, asking me to go in in a few days' time for an operation to remove a lump from my throat. I no longer had to anticipate the agony of sitting in front of my computer on the first day of my retreat, wondering how on earth to begin. Instead I needed to prepare for a stay in hospital—for my throat to be cut open and a lump taken out. Apparently there was a slight risk that my voice would be left hoarse. How odd, to be in danger of losing my voice when I'd hardly begun to find it!

A Trip to Greece

Shanti was in her last year at school. I wanted to do something with her, something to mark her growing up and our changing relationship. I thought we could go off on an adventure together; it might be a chance to get to know one another a little better, away from home, before she finally left.

We decided to go to Greece, and bring to life her study of classical civilization.

We got off to a bad start. Having just come out of hospital, I was in a slightly depressed state, and Shanti, usually renowned for her delightful excitement when anticipating things to come, was missing her boyfriend, who had gone away to university; she admitted that the pain of parting had diminished her pleasure in what was to come.

I wondered how we would get on, away from our normal environment; perhaps we would find we had little to say to one another. I was sure I would feel over-responsible for how everything went, even for how much Shanti enjoyed herself. I worried about arranging travel and accommodation, but I tried to assume an air of confidence.

On arrival in Athens, at one-thirty in the morning, I was glad I'd been persuaded to book a hotel for the night. However, our taxi driver wouldn't allow us to stay there; he said the street was very bad, and so he drove on until he'd found us a room in a respectable part of town.

Thankful and relieved, we unlocked the door. It was dark inside—even with the light on. The room was small and the ceiling was high; the furnishings were dull, the wallpaper grey, mouldy, and peeling. Any dream we'd had of comfort, of whitewashed walls, a balcony, and a view was shattered—this was more like a prison cell.

We didn't intend to go on as we'd started, but our first impressions of Athens, on top of our low spirits, were too strong for us to withstand.

We certainly had an adventure, but it wasn't quite the one we'd planned. One night, I was woken by my nearly-eighteen-year-old daughter crying, 'Mum! There's a mosquito!' I did feel over-responsible and I had to try and stop myself. I wanted to be a confident, worldly-wise mother, but I wasn't.

When we were returning to our hotel from visiting the Acropolis, I led Shanti on a wild-goose chase. I was trying to find the city gates and eventually realized I was following a map from the fifth century BCE! Shanti was annoyed with me. I wished her adventurous spirit could have risen to the challenge; then she might have laughed at my mistake. Back inside our gloomy room we were faced with the stark fact that although we were on holiday we were feeling pretty miserable. The following day Shanti didn't want to get up; she'd been dreaming that we were back at home.

After a tiring morning and a frustrating search for lunch, we ended up in the National Gardens. We found a shady square, occupied in one corner by an elderly couple. As we tucked into our picnic of fresh bread and yogurt, we relaxed and our spirits lifted. A man came into the square and seemed to walk deliberately in our direction. I made sure my dress was decent and glanced at Shanti, whose knees were well displayed. He walked past us and out of the square. 'Harmless after all,' I thought, until I saw that he had circled round us and was back again. He sat down on a bench, half-hidden from us behind a tree and once more I assumed that he was innocent. But the next time I happened to glance his way I exclaimed 'Oh, my goodness!' Shanti said I sounded shocked—I was. He had moved out from behind the tree and was now displaying a large, erect penis. We packed away the remains of our lunch and left.

Back in our dismal hotel room I couldn't hold back my tears. On top of everything I was premenstrual and I couldn't help being affected by Shanti's predominant mood. I was too dependent on her happiness for my own. I confessed that I had begun to wonder whether we should try to shorten our holiday from two weeks to one. It would be dreadful to carry on as we had been doing. Shanti was overjoyed at my suggestion; we could go all out to enjoy ourselves in the time we had left. But when we discovered that a return flight could not be confirmed until an hour before the plane left and that we would have to live in uncertainty for the remainder of the week, she sank back into misery. Eventually I threatened to go sightseeing alone, and for a while she cheered up.

On the bus to Delphi an English couple were studying their map of Greece. I plucked up courage, and when the man began to fold it up I asked if I could borrow it. I felt a strange longing for the couple to take an interest in us, even to take us under their wing. When I returned the map and hardly received an acknowledgement, let alone my imagined response, I didn't mind; I wanted to show Shanti that I could cope, that I was confident, that I was a grown-up mother.

In a smart restaurant we drank tea overlooking the valley and the mountains. The peace was gently disturbed by the Americans sitting nearby. When asked what he would like to be doing whilst the women went shopping for presents, one of the men replied, 'I'd like to be at home.' Shanti felt for him—he was a lot further away than we were. I envied them their companionship.

From our balcony we could see the sea. I suggested a trip down there for a swim. We arrived at the seafront: a small harbour with a long stretch of cafés on the wide promenade, but no beach. We walked on into the suburbs of the town, following signs to the 'beach camp'. Everywhere was deserted: not only was it lunchtime, it was also out of season, a ghost town. We turned down a pathway, still imagining we might find our stretch of golden sand. Could that be a beach, way down there? We walked on until there was no mistaking it. Between the road and the sea a two-metre wide beach of gravel and rubbish was what the tourist guide had referred to as 'attracting many bathers'. Perhaps it looked different in the summer.

Back at the harbour we had two hours to wait for the bus. We walked along the seafront and sat down on a bench. An old man came along on his bicycle. He stopped at our bench and began to unload plastic carrier bags of shopping from the handlebars. He indicated that he'd like to sit down, hoping that we wouldn't mind. I glanced up and down the promenade, noticing that the benches on either side of us were empty. Why had he chosen to stop here? We would see. He reeled off the names of a few countries to see where we came from, shoved a pomegranate into Shanti's hands and began to unravel a fishing line. It was rather a primitive procedure and I was fascinated. As he unravelled he tried out the famous names on us— Plato, Socrates. He was a harmless, friendly old man. He began fumbling about in his carrier bag, leaned across Shanti to thrust a pomegranate upon me and proceeded to stroke Shanti's leg. I gathered up my daughter and we walked away.

There were some good moments: Shanti's quiet euphoria as we wandered around the Acropolis; sitting in the theatre of Dionysus, eating grapes and imagining all those years ago; relaxing in cafés; discovering that Delphi was a village on a hillside and nothing like Athens, and that our hotel room was the one we'd dreamed of; contemplating the ancient ruins when the other tourists had gone to lunch; and a vibrant meeting with the bronze Charioteer. But still Shanti wanted to go home.

We went straight to the airport from Delphi, and had four hours to wait when we got there. We drank coffee, ate the remains of our bread and cheese, and got caught up in the intrigues of other people's lives. Finally it was time to check in, and for me to ask for George. He took our tickets and passports and told us to wait. Shanti's face fell when she realized we still hadn't got a definite answer. At last George returned and casually said 'That's OK'. He had no idea how anxious we'd been, and was gone before he saw us hugging each other, trembling with excitement and relief, like a couple of schoolgirls. The ordeal was over. We were going home.

Shanti Leaves Home

Shanti had applied to university to do a combined course in English and art history. The only place she was offered was for a course that didn't appeal to her. Later, when she applied through the clearing house, the courses advertised were mostly for science subjects, and her future as a student looked highly unlikely.

A 'year out' had once sounded attractive, but the harsh reality was now apparent—jobs were not easy to find and she probably couldn't afford to leave home—so she had made up her mind to go straight to college.

Eventually, with just a week to go before the start of term, she was accepted for a course in visual cultures at Derby. She was so happy and excited and relieved—and so was I. I spent the evening on the phone trying to borrow a car so that we could go to Derby the next day and find Shanti somewhere to live.

By twelve o'clock, in great excitement, we were on our way. We arrived in Derby to find there was a housing crisis, and we were warned not to be choosy because some students would inevitably be ending up with a mattress but no room to call their own. The house-hunting procedure, it appeared, was disorganized and extremely time-consuming, and our high spirits were crushed. With extraordinary good luck, however, within an hour we had found Shanti a house which she would share with three others.

Three and a half hours later we were back in Norwich, in time for Shanti to meet her friends at the pub. She was bursting to share her news with them. Inevitably some of her closest friends were so shocked at the suddenness of her impending departure that they were more upset than pleased for her, and she came home having been unable to celebrate.

The next question to figure out was how to get her and all her belongings up to Derby the following weekend. Assuming that term would be starting later, I had moved an important meeting forward to ensure that I would be around if she did go to university. Now my meeting and her departure would clash. Sona, too, would be away. She thought a friend might drive her up, and if necessary she would go by train and I could take her things a few days later.

Unfortunately the friend couldn't oblige. I wondered if I could shorten my meeting. I didn't want her to set off for her new life, alone, with only as many of her belongings as she could carry. After all the talk the previous year of her leaving home, suddenly she was going; and now that the excitement and relief of her being accepted at university had died down, I was feeling the sadness of it. I had to see her off properly—I had to find a way of taking her myself.

I had at first assumed that it simply couldn't be done. I had a prior, very important, engagement within the Sangha. As commitment to the Three Jewels was of primary and life-style of secondary importance, the responsibilities I had taken on as a result of going for Refuge should take precedence over those I had towards my family. But once again I had taken a superficial and simplistic view. It seemed

I still hadn't stopped separating my spiritual life from my life as a mother. It was perhaps easier to do that than to figure out how to honour all of my responsibilities.

I was due to spend a few days in Shropshire, with the other Dharmacharinis responsible for the ordination process, and we would be deciding whom we would be recommending for ordination that year. It was impossible to rearrange my meeting. But I also knew that I dearly wanted to take Shanti to Derby and that it was important for both of us that I did. If I cut short my stay in Shropshire I could be home in time to take her.

On the way back I travelled via London to borrow my mother's car, and then had a nightmare journey up to Norwich. The car had recently been checked over at the garage but even so there was something wrong. A red light flickered, the temperature gauge was rising, and the lights seemed to be dimming. I didn't dare stop at the side of the road, in the dark, miles from anywhere.

I arrived home at one o'clock in the morning, in an AA van, with the car in tow.

I lay awake unable to sleep: I felt guilty for having lied, in my panic, to the AA, and for having worried my mother sick. And now I had to figure out how to get another car in time to leave for Derby at nine-thirty that same morning.

The gods were with us and my second try, at eight forty-five on Sunday morning, was successful. At ten o'clock Shanti and I set off with what appeared to be the entire contents of her bedroom.

As we drove away from Norwich Shanti said her eyes wouldn't stop watering. I assumed it was due to tiredness as she had just had two very late nights. But no, she said, it was the pain of leaving that was affecting her.

We arrived a little later than planned but in time for Shanti to sign the contract. The other three students were there, along with their parents and one or two brothers and sisters. We looked around, talked about what needed doing, and had a cup of tea. Joanne said she wanted the middle bedroom, Corrie didn't mind, and Shanti was only too happy—after having lived in a tiny room for so long—to take the largest one at the front. Steve had already agreed to Mr Davis's light-heartedly put, but serious, suggestion that he should occupy the downstairs front room, as a sort of protective device.

We unloaded the car and as Shanti took box after box up to her room she began to feel embarrassed. However, she was still glad she'd brought everything—better to have too much than too little, she said.

When the car was empty we stood in her room—already transformed by the great pile of her belongings. My job was done; it was time to leave her to it. But I wanted to help her to settle in. I hung the curtains up and she made the bed. She didn't want to unpack anything else so I suggested we explore the town a bit. My suggestion was a mistake. I had wanted to delay the parting, but I just got irritable driving around. I was worn out.

I left her at the phone box talking to her boyfriend. By the time I'd reached the motorway, tears were running down my cheeks and I cried and cried.

Just Visiting

After two weeks in Derby Shanti came home for a weekend. I got very excited about seeing her. It was strange for her to be coming home but just visiting. Sundari and I had been getting used to living without her. It was a novelty for us all.

I wanted to know how Shanti had been getting on and what she'd been doing. How was her house working out? Did she have what she needed for her room? Was she eating properly? How was she getting to and from the campus? Did she need more sheets? I wanted to know, I wanted to help, I wanted to organize, I wanted to make everything all right. I was fussing. I listened to her talking about not going home at night because it was easier to sleep on friends' floors —and safer when she'd heard how rough her neighbourhood was, full of drugs and guns. I listened to her describing the best night out she had had—a hypnosis show for the Freshers. All I could do was listen. It was another world and I had to let her go. If she wanted sheets, she could ask.

She said she was eating very well. She didn't like having meat cooked in the house, but then the others had to put up with something too. Slightly shamefaced, Shanti admitted she was still smoking —but it wasn't a habit! I wondered why I minded so much. I was obviously concerned for her health. Did I want my values to be her values? Did I want to feel I had influence, even control, over her? I'd had little control for years. I listened to her talk and felt a bit awkward and empty. But I was glad to see her happy.

Later on a friend came to visit her. I lay awake, annoyed by the sound of voices, and at midnight I called down.

The next day Shanti was busy meeting friends and buying books for college. I had been looking forward to seeing a little more of her. At last she came home; but her friends would be round soon to take her out for a meal. The phone kept ringing, always for her, and then someone turned up early. There was no time now for us to have a quiet cup of tea together. I couldn't hide my disappointment. I got annoyed that she hadn't washed up her coffee cups and I asked her to make sure her friends were quiet if they came back at night. She huffed at me indignantly. I went up to my room and might have cried if the next phone call hadn't been for me. It was Bhante ringing to say that he was happy with the recommendations from the ordination team and that I should go ahead and invite all thirteen women to the ordination retreat.

I printed out thirteen copies of a previously prepared letter. Delight, anticipation of the event to come, and anxiety as to whether I would catch the post were now added to my agitation.

When I returned from the Post Office the sitting-room was full of giggling girls and boys, arguing loudly over trivia. I wanted them gone. Shanti was now regretting that she was going out and would have no time to spend with me. Then she surprised me by asking for money. She had been so conscientious about saving in preparation for having to live off a meagre grant, aware that I would be in no position to support her. And now, it seemed, she had taken on the poor student attitude of feeling obliged to scrounge from home. I was disappointed, and yet, aware that I had been unclear as to how much I could help her, I couldn't really blame her for trying. I thought of my own parents, and with a feeling of shame I thought that perhaps I too, in a more subtle way, still 'scrounged from home'. I still wanted to be looked after, and I still wanted to look after my daughter.

Shanti left early the next morning to go back to Derby and I left time to heal my hurt.

Everything was Wrong

I had just settled down to write about the experience of my daughter leaving home when the telephone rang. It was Shanti. She wanted to come home—for good!

Everything was wrong—even her course, which until now had appeared to be the one thing that had kept her going through other difficulties. Something must have happened, I thought. It was only three days ago that she had left Norwich, after her second weekend home, saying she was looking forward to getting back to old Derby. I knew she got lonely, that her house wasn't much to speak of, that she lived in a rough area and quite far from the campus. I was a bit concerned about her drinking and smoking. Was there anything else I didn't know about? Yes, she said.

I wanted to go up and see her but she wouldn't have it. She insisted on coming home, so I told her it would be to talk and not to go out with her friends.

Sundari was not happy; first at the thought that I might go to Derby and spend yet another night away from home, and then she was angry at the possibility of Shanti moving back. She took it out on me. Upset by her reaction, after we'd been getting on so well together, I found it hard not to snap back at her.

Shanti and I had a good talk, but she was left thinking I wasn't 'on her side'. I felt hurt that she had assumed she knew my opinion when I was still trying to form it. Too late I realized she was desperate for support of her proposed action. Any questioning she took as disapproval. She was trying to leave home but she still needed me. Mother and daughter—we weren't yet ready for more sophisticated communication and understanding of one another.

I never discovered exactly what else had gone wrong in Derby, except that it was some sort of boyfriend trouble.

Doors Slammed

For her seventeenth birthday Sundari wanted a CD player. It was the only thing she really wanted. Although I thought it extravagant, I wanted her to have what she wanted. I wanted her to have what she wanted because she was my daughter, because I felt a pressure to provide, and because I didn't want to bear the brunt of her reaction if she was disappointed.

I had thought that between us Sona and I could contribute towards it, but she'd have to find more money herself. I allowed her to remain hopeful before I'd talked with Sona. When he said he could only give her half of what she'd hoped for, she got upset, and then furious.

Shanti had just arrived home with all her belongings. The calm and clear atmosphere that Sundari and I had established was now replaced with tension and confusion.

I asked Sona to be patient with Sundari. I realized, rather guiltily, that I had been hoping that he, father, would make everything all right. I was due to go out and I didn't want to leave the girls as they were—Sundari upset and moody about her birthday present, on top of being seriously put out by Shanti's coming home, and Shanti relieved to be home and wanting to settle in again, but aware that her presence wasn't altogether welcomed. Then my mother rang, ill and thoroughly miserable, desperate to share with me her worries about my sister and her children since her husband had left with another woman. She told me how my niece had come downstairs, unable to sleep, crying 'I want my daddy'. I could have cried too.

I listened to my mother until I simply had to go. I left Sundari in a heap on the floor, Shanti sorting out her boxes, and Sona still hurt by Sundari's behaviour.

At my Order meeting someone suggested getting a second-hand player. I tried to believe that that was the answer.

I arrived home to find the girls and a friend of Shanti's watching television. I used to come home to just Sundari and we'd have a little chat. Now I felt out of place, a bit resentful of the friend, and I took myself up to my room. The friend soon left and Sundari went to her room. I decided to put the question to her. As I'd thought, it wasn't an answer: she'd set her heart on a new one. But now, she said, Dad wasn't going to give her any money, and she crumpled up into a heap on her bed and sobbed. I left her to it, but wondered every now and again whether the loud sobs meant she wanted me to go in and talk to her. I decided I wasn't up to taking the risk of being rudely rejected. Doors slammed and she thundered down the stairs. I nearly rushed after her to forbid such behaviour. For a moment I could have thrown her out of the house. But I reminded myself that the issue was loaded, that I had my own part to play in it, and that moods change.

I didn't see her in the morning. I heard her singing and felt relieved. When she'd left the house I felt the strain and I cried, and later I snapped at Shanti for her unmindful behaviour.

Back to Three

After only seven weeks away Shanti had returned home. Sundari and I had been enjoying having the house to ourselves and she had admitted that she liked living with just me. After a long history of rubbing each other up the wrong way, we had been getting on extremely well.

We had been prepared for Shanti to come home during the holidays, but we hadn't been prepared for her to move back so soon. Sundari was really quite put out and couldn't help showing her displeasure. Shanti was in a very raw, sensitive state. She had been struggling for some time. There was nothing worthwhile left to keep her going in Derby, and yet she hated the idea of being a drop-out. She had finally made her decision and now she had to face the consequences. She was relieved to be home but she was extremely touchy. Any talk about what she had done or was going to do she took as criticism. She thought everyone would regard her as a failure. She desperately wanted to be welcomed home, and yet it was obvious that Sundari and I weren't exactly overjoyed to have her.

We all had to readjust and we did it with some reluctance. The girls quarrelled. I was disturbed and upset by the added noise, chaos, and tension in the house. I was particularly upset that Sundari and I seemed to have lost the delight in each other's company that we had experienced whilst Shanti was away.

A welcome respite came when my sister asked Shanti to help her out during the last busy week of term. Sundari and I were soon to go off to India and so we now had more space in which to prepare ourselves. I was relieved to find that our former good relations were quickly restored.

After taking Shanti to Greece, I had wondered what I would do with Sundari. The only suggestions she could come up with were Casablanca, as it sounded like a sun-drenched beach, or one of the fashion centres of the world—she dreamt of jumping into a black taxi, arms laden with expensive carrier bags. I was therefore very pleasantly surprised when she responded positively to my suggestion that she come with me to India. I had been afraid she might be too wary of snakes and biting insects. She did worry about all sorts of things, but with me with her she felt she would be safe enough.

I was glad I'd planned our trip at this time rather than a year later. Shanti would have a chance to settle in at home without feeling in the way, and Sundari and I would have a chance to establish our relationship on a more mature and sturdy basis.

We turned our attention to our forthcoming adventure. Sundari wanted every possible precautionary injection, and we had to find suitable clothing. I borrowed several Punjabi suits from a friend. Sundari had great fun dressing up in them and she ended up with a decent, if somewhat glamorous, wardrobe.

We were both concerned about Shanti, hoping she would be all right on her own over Christmas. She had already thrown herself into the job of reapplying to university, having decided she wanted to become a teacher. After all the stress of leaving Derby and now this rush of activity she might soon find herself at a loss, and with us both away might become lonely and depressed. But, we reflected, she was a big girl, she'd taken her first step away from home and, having tripped over, she was now picking herself up to start again.

I was glad that Shanti would be at home. It meant that when Sundari returned from India, three weeks before me (Sinhadevi was joining me for the second part of my visit), it wouldn't be to an empty house. And yet my mind was not completely at rest. I wondered how they would get on. I wasn't afraid of rowdy parties—I knew neither of them wanted to risk any damage to our home. Sundari had taken on a rather possessive attitude to the house whilst Shanti had been away and no longer regarded her older sister as having any real rights within it. When she got back Shanti would have had the house to herself for two weeks. She liked having her friends staying until all hours of the morning whereas, when Sundari was ready for bed, she wanted everyone to go home. Shanti had got used to doing as she wished and Sundari, with her big sister out of the way, had become more confident in asserting herself. I tried to get them to consider one another a little more and to work things out together, but they found it very difficult to do so.

Sundari's stay in India proved to be more successful than I'd hoped. I had thought she might be rather dependent on me, but she was happy just knowing I was around. For the most part she was very pleasant company, and when I was experiencing difficulties, her cheerfulness and buoyancy were of great comfort. It really did seem as though we had at last firmly cemented the good feelings between us.

The only trouble we had was on Christmas Day. Lokamitra had taken us, with his family and his wandering friend, Jyotipala, for a few days by the sea. We ate our picnic lunch *en route* —bread and cheese, salad, bananas, and Christmas cake—under the shade of a tree at the edge of a rice-field. In the late afternoon we were swimming in the Arabian Sea. As we drove back to our guest house Sundari and Jyotipala (an ex-Trappist from Yorkshire), both marvelling that it was Christmas Day, treated us to a concert of their favourite Christmas songs.

Back at the guest house Sundari and I planned to settle into our room before supper. The room was large with a high ceiling, a wash-basin, and three iron-framed beds. It was rather stark after the relative comfort we'd been used to, and the cosiness of the apartment that the others were occupying. Feeling pretty exhausted after our journey, and premenstrual, I wasn't looking forward to the laborious task of rigging up our mosquito nets. I wondered whether we should bother. I saw that a mood had descended on Sundari. She didn't like the room and she certainly wouldn't sleep in it without the security of a net. Back in Poona she had identified very much with her bed. She would climb underneath the net, at any time of day, even with no mosquitoes about, and settle down with her book, her diary, or her music. It was her own little room within the room she shared with me. But now she didn't feel comfortable, even with me by her side, in this big, bare, dormitory-like room, with the rest of our party way down the corridor, and other families, speaking a foreign language, in the rooms all around us. We had only been in the country a few days and we were both, I realized, feeling quite insecure. I needed Sundari's cheerful presence to motivate me. Fortunately, inspiration soon came to her—we could use the garlands we'd been given at the hostel to tie up our nets! For a while she set to with some enthusiasm, determined that at least her bed should be safe from creepy-crawlies. But the string broke and the cupboard door we'd used to fasten it to kept swinging open. She gave up. Tired, irritable, and upset by her mood, I forced myself to keep going and finally managed to hang the nets.

When we settled into bed that night, knowing that Sundari was still miserable, I asked her if she was OK. It had been the worst Christmas Day of her life, she said—banana sandwiches for lunch and no presents!

On the way back to Poona Sundari redeemed herself of her bad mood. We were all feeling ill from driving along the winding roads. Rajyashri, my two-year-old niece, had finally fallen asleep and so I took her in my arms to allow Ranjana to move to the front. But Rajyashri's slumber was not deep enough to prevent her being disturbed and she wasn't pleased to be removed from her mother's lap. She cried, she shouted, and she kicked. As she cried her shoe came off and that was something else to cry about. Ranjana reached out to hold her hand but that wasn't good enough. She fought to escape me as I held her tight. Any attempt to distract her was in vain. We were all so tired and irritable, we could do no more, and we resigned ourselves to her cries. Then, in the midst of our gloom, Sundari, as though struck by divine inspiration, suddenly burst into song. In a fit of exasperation she was trying to drown Rajyashri's yelling, and the effect was remarkable. Rajyashri stared at Sundari, who was singing at the top of her voice and pretending to be a monkey. Then Ashok joined in with an elephant song, and when it came to 'Old Macdonald's Farm', Jyotipala and I were singing too. The back of the jeep was transformed. We were all singing our hearts out and Rajyashri had completely forgotten her troubles. Later on, when Sundari had returned to England, Rajyashri's eyes would light up with delight when she was reminded of 'Sundari's song'.

On my return from India I was touched to find that the girls were both genuinely happy to have me home. I had thought it might have been my turn to feel in the way. We all, once again, had some re-adjusting to do. They seemed to accept me back much more quickly and easily than I was able to re-establish myself. I couldn't bear seeing bagfuls of empty beer cans and wine bottles left outside the back door, and cigarette ends strewn on the path—though I was thankful they'd upheld my rule of not letting friends smoke indoors. I didn't want to hear their constant music or have the television dominate the sitting-room. They had got used to clearing up when it suited them rather than with anyone else in mind. I tried not to complain or nag or order them about. They thought themselves too adult for that sort of treatment. They listened to my pleas, but still didn't act. Having left them to themselves quite a bit over the last few years I had given them a certain amount of independence and encouraged them to take more responsibility. Much as I wanted to be in control of my own household, I couldn't be. I had left them to it, now I had to fit in.

I wanted a quiet time in which to adjust to being back in England as well as back at home. But gone were the days when I could rely on school hours for some peace. Shanti had no particular programme to her day and was often in. Sundari's sixth-form college didn't require her to remain on the premises when she didn't have classes, and she seemed to have rather a lot of free time. At any moment I could expect her to burst into my room wanting to know what I thought of her hairstyle or the clothes she was wearing. Sometimes she would simply come and stand in front of my mirror—in spite of the fact that she had a full-length one in her own room. She seemed to want somebody else to notice how beautiful she was. She might ask me something or tell me something, and the more I drew her attention to the fact that I was busy, the more she prattled on. Sometimes I got exasperated with her, but I didn't get cross. I knew that if I wanted any decent communication with Sundari, it had to be on her terms and whenever she was ready for it. I wanted to make the most of her when she was in such a friendly mood. She was irresistible. But I couldn't always stop whatever I was doing for her, even though that might have been easier than the great effort involved in getting rid of her, after which I would still be disturbed because she would get upset or at least pretend to be so.

Time and time again, over the years, I had been in the same situation. I had tended to think that as a mother I should be available whenever wanted or needed. And often I wanted to be needed. But even when I didn't feel like being available I couldn't lock my door. It was as though I habitually listened out for the baby's cry. But the babies were now grown, and if I wanted to work I had to shut them out. I had to be clear and determined, and prepared both to enjoy and to suffer the consequences. I simply had to be firmer with Sundari and I made a rule that I must not be disturbed whilst working in my room in the mornings.

Shanti had had no luck with her university applications. She had been for one interview, at Ripon, and she was waiting to hear from them. I came home from a few days away to find her in a sorry state. I assumed she'd been rejected. She had, but not yet by the university—her boyfriend had finished with her. A week later she telephoned Ripon. They had at last made their decision and unfortunately they couldn't accept her.

The three of us were looking ahead to leaving home, to leaving the comfort and security of the home we'd made for ourselves over the past twenty years. Shanti had set the ball rolling. She had had a trial run and we were all affected by it. Now we each looked ahead to our future with varying degrees of excitement and anxiety.

When first home Shanti had wanted to move out again as soon as she could. She wanted to be free to have her friends round whenever she liked. She wanted a bigger room. She didn't want to be nagged at for not clearing up the mess she made. But after living in a cold, gloomy, battered house in Derby, she appreciated what she had and stayed.

Sundari said that as soon as she was eighteen she would live in a shared house with some of her friends. I didn't believe she really would. I didn't think she was ready to look after herself. She wouldn't eat well—but she didn't now, and she was healthy. She wouldn't get down to her college work—but she hardly did now. She would miss the comfort and security of her own home—but she would have to fend for herself sooner or later. I imagined she would miss me—but she could always come and visit. Perhaps I wasn't ready for her to go.

I had often dreamt of the time when I would be free from the most arduous stretch of motherhood. Free to leave home. For the past nineteen years I had been running a race, and it was now a struggle to keep on going. Over the last few years I had been making a great effort to run at a steady pace, determined to see the race through as best I could without giving in to the temptation to stop and rest or take a short cut. Returning home from India I experienced a lot of conflict. Whilst there I had caught the most tangible glimpse of the finishing line that I'd ever seen. The end was in sight and I found it so hard not to succumb to the frustration which arises from wanting to leave home prematurely. I had been far away from home and from my duties as a mother. I had seen what my future could hold in store for me and I wanted it there and then. I wanted to break loose from whatever held me back. It took me some time to acknowledge the fact, once again, that I would only be free if I saw my commitment through.

With a quiet mind
Come into that empty house,
your heart,
And feel the joy of the way
Beyond the world.

nine

Moving Towards Brahmacharya

I was used to not seeing a great deal of Subhuti. He led a very busy life and was often out of the country. Once we had acknowledged that our relationship was more than a casual affair we occasionally managed a holiday abroad.

In Spain Subhuti diagnosed me as suffering from Gothic sickness—the disease which comes about from getting overwhelmed. I was at my worst in Gothic cathedrals where, feeling small and insignificant and unable to focus on any one thing I would sometimes feel so sick and dizzy that I would have to sit down, or better still get right out of the building. Having diagnosed me Subhuti practised his new-found knowledge of neurolinguistic programming on me and I found some relief. In Venice I learnt to visit an art gallery without succumbing. And by the time we went to Florence I was able to work out for myself how much I could handle in the Uffizi.

If a holiday can be called divine then such indeed was our stay in Florence. It was the most romantic of our trips abroad and it was the last of its kind. I gazed out of the attic window, across the orange-tiled roofs glinting in the evening sunlight, and a touch of melancholy overcame me. Was I really on my way to giving up this most perfect affair?

From the very start the end had been in sight, or at least in mind. Despite Subhuti's ready acceptance of my proposition, he wanted, ideally, to lead a celibate life and become an *anagarika* (literally a homeless one). He was strongly attracted to *brahmacharya*. At times it was very clear how much he wanted to resist the insistent demand of sexual desire, convinced that if he could free himself from it he would be more deeply content and have more energy available for the pursuit of his real heart's desire. When, after a year or so, he took a vow of celibacy for a year, I was disappointed but not unprepared. Left with neither a husband nor a lover I began to consider the life for myself. I even got so far as to wonder whether I could become an *anagarika* whilst I still lived at home with my children. Two older women were shortly to be taking on the *brahmacharya* precept and so becoming *anagarikas*. I attended the ceremony and, as I listened attentively to Bhante's explanation of the significance of what was being undertaken, I expected to be further inspired. But instead of a warm glow of inspiration, I felt a cold shiver run down my spine. I couldn't help thinking in terms of loss rather than gain. No, I suddenly realized, I wasn't yet ready for that. It was therefore a tremendous relief when, at the end of the year, Subhuti acknowledged the same.

We could never forget, however, that an end had to come. Bhante had suggested that by the age of forty Order members should be seriously considering celibacy and moving towards *brahmacharya*. By the time Subhuti was almost there Bhante, so understanding of human nature, happened incidentally to move the age on to forty-five!

For one reason or another my own attraction towards *brahmacharya* was not as ardent as Subhuti's; and I couldn't just put it down to being younger than him! I couldn't help, however, being influenced by him. I supported his aspiration, and wished my own heart was more fully behind it. When he said he thought he was too fond of me I didn't want to understand but really I did. He had become extremely important to me. I found it hard to envisage how we would relate when such a basic element of our relationship was gone. I didn't want to lose Subhuti as a friend, and I couldn't disentangle the friend from the lover. Perhaps, I tried to comfort myself, we would be like angels, satisfied by a mere glance.

When my island retreat came to an end—by which time Subhuti and I had been in our relationship for about eleven years—I felt much happier in myself. I had had time to focus and reflect on the changes that were going on in my life. I felt more whole, less in need, less desperate about my supposed lack of friendship, and less dependent on Subhuti. When he told me that he was planning to go and live abroad for a few years, I was therefore able, after the initial shock, sincerely to wish him well. I felt a bit sad for myself that he wouldn't be so close at hand, but how could I not rejoice in what was so obviously a good move for him? Our meetings would necessarily be fewer and farther between. It would be a good opportunity to work more consciously towards *brahmacharya* and to experiment with definite periods of celibacy. I responded to the challenge. After all I was now forty and I had been thinking much more seriously about it all.

Even if at times I chose to forget what I was aspiring to, Bhante would be ready with a reminder. At a gathering of the Order he commented on the suit I was wearing. It was the same colour as that of the robes of the old monks in Burma, he said, with a twinkle in his eye. OK, I thought, I'm on my way, but I'm not that close. There was more, however, to come. The main speaker of the day was Kamalashila and his subject was 'Sex, Addiction, and Freedom'. First he led us through a detailed account of the facts of life. Then he vividly portrayed how sex was at the root of so much suffering—from the anguish of waiting for the telephone to ring through to the horror and bloodshed of crimes of passion, and war. He offered us the alternative of a life cultivating positive aloneness—a freedom from need-based relationships. A life less and less preoccupied with sense desire and more and more inspired by the example of the Buddhas and Bodhisattvas. A life wholeheartedly devoted to the development of insight into the nature of Reality, and compassion for all living beings. A life dedicated to the attainment of Enlightenment. By the end of his talk I felt as though I hadn't a leg to stand on. How could I defend my desire for a relationship based on sex to go on *ad infinitum*? Must I confess to addiction? How could I not be inspired by the vision of *brahmacharya*?

I met with Subhuti before he moved away. I was finally ready to discuss, more openly and honestly than I'd wanted to before, what I'd known all along—that our relationship, as a sexual relationship, had no future. We were not going to build a world around it. We were not going to get married and have children. I had never wanted that, although I did confess to having had the occasional fantasy of us living together. I even confessed that I had once imagined I could be happy, like Dora in *David Copperfield*, simply holding his pencils for him! But, no, no matter how much I loved Subhuti, I couldn't centre my world on him; it wouldn't have been good for either of us. We were not, we admitted, in control of the casual affair we had embarked on. It was now controlling us. Sex had given both pleasure and pain: intimacy, affection, love; attachment, longing, and clinging. In traditional Buddhist terms, feeling had led on to craving, and the Wheel of Life was sent spinning round again. I could deny it no longer, my sexual relationship with Subhuti was holding me back from a more wholehearted pursuit of my true goal. To deliberately maintain it now would be to strengthen the bonds of attachment, to bind ourselves more tightly to the ever-revolving Wheel. I felt the sparks of real inspiration and without waiting for Subhuti to take the initiative, as previously I would have done, I offered a suggestion as to how we should proceed.

When we parted, we were aware that our night spent together might well have been our last. It wasn't—but it was definitely the beginning of the end. The way ahead seemed so much clearer now that I too was sure of where I was going. It was as though we had finally joined forces in our efforts. For me the balance had tipped. I could now wholeheartedly support Subhuti's aspiration because it was what I too honestly wanted.

We wanted to maintain our good feelings for one another; we wanted friendship to triumph over desire. I was determined we should succeed. I felt sure that our concern for one another, our 'love', went beyond the bonding of sex. Or was it that that was what I wanted to believe? How could I really be sure until we'd been put to the test? I was prepared for a difficult and perhaps painful time as we brought one aspect of our relationship to an end, and I could only have faith that it would be worth it. I couldn't know what the eventual outcome would be. I appreciated that in the end I would gain, but from my present point of view I still couldn't refrain from thinking in terms of loss. I wanted to continue seeing as much of Subhuti as I possibly could, which wasn't going to be a great deal, but I wondered whether he might prefer that we kept apart. Subhuti, however, was keen to keep in touch and I was so glad. I was deeply moved by his concern that having come this far in association with one another we should work hand in hand, as it were, to achieve the goal that we both wanted. That way we were more likely to succeed and to avoid the pain and resentment which so often follow the ending of a sexual relationship.

As anticipated it wasn't easy. We were celibate for almost a year and then the time came to review our efforts. I knew that my resolve had weakened. There was no ignoring the dreadful day but perhaps we could put it off a little longer. Without the discipline of a vow we were now faced with a question and it was our lower natures that answered it.

Oh, how glorious it was to dissolve into one another's arms once again! And yet what was that nagging feeling that now disturbed the clarity of our communication? We had once again tasted the fruit of sensual delight and craving had been reawakened.

Acknowledging that for the time being sex still had a place in our lives, the next step, before dispensing with it altogether, was to insist that that place was a very peripheral one. If we were going to continue to meet we should consciously focus more attention on other areas of common interest. We decided to experiment with spending some time away together, on a sort of working holiday. Subhuti was in the middle of writing a book, and I welcomed an opportunity to further the writing I'd initiated when on my island retreat. In the autumn of 1993 we packed up our computers and met in France.

It was quite a struggle for me to get going but with Subhuti's encouragement and steady support as he tapped away in another room, I eventually settled down. We went for walks in the afternoons, gathered chestnuts and roasted them on the fire.

The time had come for another review and a discussion on our strategy for the future. In the midst of so idyllic a sojourn we were both a little reluctant to put an end to such times. Should we grasp the nettle and name a day? I was planning to go away, to be very much on my own, for a year starting the following summer. It would make sense for that time to be a celibate time for me. It would make sense if it was the beginning of a life of *brahmacharya*. But right then I couldn't help admitting that I thought I could quite happily proceed with a little indulgence every now and again. We knew what we ought to do but still we didn't quite want to. We agreed to another period of celibacy and then we'd see.

I began to wonder whether I'd taken on too much. I was in the process of letting go of my daughters as they stretched their wings and ventured forth from home. It was proving to be more difficult than I'd imagined. I had taken the attitude 'In for a penny, in for a pound'. I thought it made sense. I was having to cut the umbilical cord which tied me to my daughters; why not free myself further and sever the bond of desire? Now I wasn't so sure. Perhaps I was giving myself too hard a time. Couldn't I hold on to the comfort of romance and an illusion of security for just a little longer? But I wasn't the only one to consider. I knew how dearly Subhuti wanted to become celibate, in spite of his own hesitations. I knew, too, of the conflict he had suffered over the years; I was now experiencing something of it myself. I recalled how I'd been prepared to be put to the test. I couldn't turn back now.

Shortly before I was due to go away we spent a few days together. We both avoided the subject. I couldn't bear the unspoken tension any longer. What *were* we going to do? There wasn't really any alternative now but to say we'd be celibate for a year and then probably that would be that. Having broached the subject an ease and clarity returned to our communication and the way ahead was once more straightforward.

A Dream and a Bright Idea

In another year Sundari would be leaving school. Could it be possible that the end of the race was actually in sight? Was I really in the middle of my final two-year stint of devoted motherhood? For a long time

I had been dreaming of going away on my own, of being free for a while of my normal responsibilities. I thought it was only a dream, a selfish longing, until a friend encouraged me to consider it seriously. Perhaps it was important, even crucial, that at this great turning point in my life I should have a complete break ... and if I did so it should be for at least a year. I consulted those I worked most closely with—the ordination team and the Mitra Convenors—and they thought it might be possible to do without me.

I decided to give Sundari six months after leaving school to settle whatever she was going to do. Then, all being well, I would go. Having made up my mind, I inevitably began to get impatient and frustrated that I couldn't go sooner. I wanted my dream to become a reality. To my surprise, Sundari came to my rescue by announcing that she was going to be an au pair in America for a year. At first I thought it was just a bright idea that would come to nothing, but she seemed serious and determined. It suited me perfectly—now I needn't wait the extra six months. I got the final go-ahead from my colleagues—they would manage without me for a year—and then I began to plan.

What would I do with myself for a whole year? There was plenty of study I wanted to do, and I had always longed for more time to meditate. But most importantly I wanted to stop and stare. I wanted to continue what I'd begun on my island retreat. I wanted to get a clearer perspective on my life. I wanted to reflect on the paths I had trodden—paths that had so often seemed contradictory, but which were now, finally, converging. I wanted to tell the story of a continuing journey from home to homelessness, from attachment to freedom. And I wanted to tell it in writing.

I wanted to get right away—somewhere abroad. My father kindly offered me the use of his house in France for the autumn, winter, and spring. It was a good size for one person, and quietly situated at the top of a hill in the tiny hamlet of Lacapelle. I would be alone in a foreign country, knowing just enough French to get by. It would be an ideal retreat—I needed to look no further.

Shanti had been trying again to get into university and this time she succeeded. I was glad. She would have had a year there by the time I went away.

Sundari was learning to drive, but apart from that she wasn't doing a lot towards finding herself a place in America. She admitted that she didn't really want to leave her boyfriend—but that wouldn't stop her from going. After hearing worrying news of a friend who was already au pairing in America, she began to think rather more seriously about the whole thing. Would she really have the patience to be with children day in and day out? What if they were horrible kids? She was quite capable of looking after children but she wasn't exactly a child-lover. She began to collect references and photographs and to fill in her forms. But she never sent them off. She came to the conclusion that she didn't want to go. I had seen it coming and thought she had probably made a wise decision. However, for me it was like having the carpet pulled from under my feet. Would I have to delay my departure after all? Then I reasoned that if she was prepared to live in America for a year without me, she could certainly manage at home or wherever. So I determined to stick to my plans. I was a bit concerned about her: she'd had enough of education for the time being, but she wasn't motivated to do anything else. She wanted something to fall into her lap—she would just have to sit at home and wait! I imagined that she would eventually get pretty bored with doing nothing and would then begin to think constructively about her future.

I had thought that once I was alone in France, I would keep my communication with the girls to a minimum. But they expected more than that and, having removed myself from them when they didn't want me to go, I thought that the least I could do was to keep in touch. In any case, I would miss them, and want to know how they were.

Leaving Home (Taking the Children with Me!)

Shanti and Sundari were planning to visit me whilst I was away. I wasn't so sure that from my point of view it would be a good idea. In the end I decided to take them with me so that we could have a holiday together before we parted. So, in July 1994, we set off for France.

I had arranged to stay for the summer months at a friend's cottage, just a couple of hours' drive away from Lacapelle. Baudet was a straggling cluster of dwellings, several miles away from any village or shop. We drove through the walnut orchard, past the grand house with a swimming-pool in its garden, up to the farm to collect the key, and then on to the end of the track to the cottage.

Despite a warning to expect rather primitive accommodation, after a long, tiring journey I was a little dismayed at the state of the place. It was to be my home for the next two months—I hoped I would soon be seduced by its charm. Fortunately the girls were just glad to be there and they took immediate pleasure in working to make it more comfortable. They were particularly concerned to clear their room of insects and barricade it against any wandering mice or mosquitoes.

When I went to offer them tea in the morning I could hardly get in for the paraphernalia stuffed into the gap beneath the door. They looked so sweet, their beds pulled close together, and their sleepy faces peeping out from under the blankets.

Their main object whilst in France appeared to be to get a good tan. They spread themselves out in the front garden, with books, drinks, and music, contentedly soaking up the sun. I quietly pottered about, settling myself in and arranging my desk and computer for when I began to write.

We took turns to cook, and we ate all our meals outside. Sometimes, when the girls had already gone inside to protect themselves from mosquitoes, I would sit on alone in the warm evening, watching the sun disappear.

Shanti experimented with the bikes; one had no brakes, the other was a man's racer. She took the racer and suggested I go for a ride with her. By the time I'd gone twenty yards, I'd had enough—the bike was a liability. I cajoled Shanti into carrying on by foot, and we would have managed a long walk if she hadn't discovered a short cut back.

I wanted to explore my surroundings but the girls were quite happy to remain in the front garden. After one more try I gave up on walks, and instead I joined them in the field playing Aero-Bee. However, I did succeed in taking them with me to a couple of *les plus beaux-villages de France.* At one, we could have gone inside a chateau, perched on the top of a hill, but, 'If you've seen one you've seen them all,' they said, and having spent many a holiday in France with my sister and her family they had seen quite a few. One of the best bits for me of a sightseeing trip was to sit in a café and watch the world go by—but they didn't even want to do that. Oh well, if they were happy simply to laze around, that was OK by me. I was enjoying just being on holiday with them—we hadn't done it very often. I was also enjoying having begun my year away.

When the time came for the girls to go, we all felt a bit loath to say goodbye. I was touched by the concern they felt, leaving me on my own. Sundari insisted I wasn't to get miserable, otherwise I should come home—and I must phone her up soon. I was glad Shanti was happy at college but I worried about Sundari—she was feeling a bit mixed about living on her own, and she still hadn't anything to do.

I took them into Brive and saw them on to the coach that would take them to London. We all put on brave faces as we waved goodbye. I drove off, following the coach down the road, and I suddenly felt very alone and sad. At the traffic-lights I caught a glimpse of them waving madly and, as we parted company, I felt a little better.

The house was so quiet without the girls, and I had to keep telling myself that it would take time for me to settle into being alone. I had looked forward to this for so long—now, perhaps inevitably, I felt somewhat at a loss. I had a lot of adjusting to do, and I would have to be patient. I couldn't believe that I was in France for a year—it was probably the opportunity of a lifetime and I wanted to make the most of it, so I determined to get going with my writing.

The weather had been too hot for me and now the rain came pouring down. It added to my loneliness and made me feel melancholy. I had to put saucepans out to catch the drips in my bedroom and I wondered how damp it might be in September. Madame, from the farm, called round to bring me some flowers. I was glad to see her and happy to have a little chat. She said the storm would be over soon, but it wasn't.

I did a little writing but other things were nagging at me. I couldn't enjoy the delights of summer in France because I had no one to share them with. I wanted to sit in cafés, drinking coffee and watching the world go by—but not on my own. I got bored with walking alone. The bike was too uncomfortable to ride. I began reading some of the numerous novels in the house and worried that I was trying to escape. I seemed to experience a constant feeling of tension, of vulnerability. I wanted to feel safe. I wondered whether I had the emotional robustness to be so on my own. I worried about Sundari and almost imagined a trip back home. I couldn't believe my mothering days were over, and I knew it would take some time for the idea to register.

Out on my walks I would come across families holidaying in their beautiful old houses and I caught myself dreaming. But the dreams didn't last.

My first letter from Sundari began, 'Dear Mum, I hope you are well. I miss you loads and hate shopping. I'm too young to be responsible.' I sympathized with her. Sometimes I wished I had someone with me who would do my shopping for me, cook for me, bring me a cup of tea in the mornings, cheer me up when I felt low, protect me from the barking dogs, rescue me if the car broke down, and guide me in this foreign land.

A Day Out

My sister and her new 'extended' family were on holiday at Caffoulens so I drove over to spend a day with them. Still feeling unsettled and vulnerable, I was looking forward to enjoying a relaxed sense of well-being and safety in the company of others. And, besides, Joanna had bought me some Earl Grey tea.

We went off to a lake to go windsurfing. I was quite happy to watch; I did have a go too, but I was frightened of falling into the cold water, and gave up before I'd really begun. That night I slept peacefully.

I decided to stay another day, then I could join in the barbecue for Emma's birthday. It started to rain, so plans for swimming were cancelled. The boys were getting on one another's nerves and a nasty quarrel broke out. It spread to include everyone but me. John drove off with his children. Joanna stormed off to cool down, leaving her two distraught. When she returned we got out a jigsaw puzzle. The strain, from undergoing the shock of recently broken marriages and unpleasant divorce proceedings, had surfaced, and now we tried to ignore it.

That night I lay awake, looking forward once again to solitude.

A Last Distraction

No matter how many times I told myself that I should settle down to being on my own, I kept imagining how nice it would be to have a friend with me. It would be such a shame to wait until later, when the summer was over. My sensible reasoning didn't stand a chance, and I set off for my evening walk in the direction of the phone box. On the way, I reassured myself that if my decision to disrupt my solitude turned out to be a mistake I should be all the more ready to be alone when the time came again.

Ten days later I drove down to Brive to meet Sinhadevi. We stopped, inevitably, on the station *terrasse* for a *café au lait*. In the warm, balmy evening the colourful neon hotel lights lent a lively, continental atmosphere to the normally rather dull town. It was almost my bedtime but I could see that it wouldn't have taken much to lure my friend off to taste the local night-life. She had crossed Paris on her way down and now suggested we might visit the city for a couple of days. After several weeks of living quietly in the country and looking ahead to months of solitude it wasn't quite what I had in mind.

In the morning I adjusted the bike and cycled down to the village for bread and croissants. I returned to find Sinhadevi sitting in her long white nightie under the ripening vines, awaiting breakfast. We ate and we talked. We talked so much I had to get the umbrella out to shield us from the midday sun.

Sinhadevi was very taken with my little retreat and she didn't mention Paris again. After the first day we worked in the mornings, helping me to establish a routine for when I was alone again. When the weather was good, and it usually was, we ate outside and lingered long over our meals. Every afternoon we went for a walk. Now, with a companion, I was more adventurous, although I was a bit put out that she wouldn't keep up with me—until she explained she had shorter legs. To her credit, however, she did nose out a café in the village where the phone box was; though once, when I'd led her a rather long and rough way round—and we were so looking forward to our *café au lait*—it was closed. We managed nevertheless to sit for many an hour in other cafés, and my longing was satisfied.

Out on our walks we gathered blackberries, apples, and damsons, (I teased my Irish friend for calling them damsels) and I cooked them up to go with ice-cream, and made them into jam to see me through the winter. We practised our rusty French together and, with a freedom of expression unimaginable in English, discovered a highly enjoyable and revealing means of communication. In our more serious moments we studied a little logic and got to grips a bit more with the mechanics of misunderstanding, realizing how full our minds were of unspoken, unexplored assumptions.

After a final *café au lait* at the station, Sinhadevi boarded her train and I drove back to Baudet. I had anticipated feeling lonely again, but I was also ready to get on with my writing, and determined to extend the routine I had established.

Wet and Miserable

I read a lot and tried to write. My body ached from sitting around so much, so I forced myself to go out for boring walks. The sky clouded over and I wanted to curl up on my bed and sleep. I wondered how long I could continue living as I was. Perhaps I would go mad. I hoped I would engage more with my writing and learn to be more disciplined. It was strange trying to recollect the past at a time in my life when I could leap into the future. I'd wanted this so badly—why did I still feel the great weight of resistance? I wondered if there was anywhere else I'd rather be or anything else I'd rather be doing. Coming up with nothing I assumed I was either contented or lacking in imagination!

The sun returned and I received a reassuring card from Sona—he was keeping an eye on Sundari. At last I was properly relaxing and enjoying living alone in my delightful abode. I persevered with my writing and told myself I was just warming up—I would really get going once I'd moved to Lacapelle.

Suddenly a premature autumn descended with a vengeance. The rain pelted down, the wind howled, and I'd never before been in the midst of so much thunder and lightning. I gathered up what decent wood I could find to make a fire, and even then I wore my coat indoors. When the ceiling above my desk began to leak I gave up trying to write and started another Jane Austen novel. The days passed by and I wondered if the sun would ever return. One morning it appeared, but Madame dampened my hopes by telling me that it had been snowing not far away.

A card arrived saying that, due to the dreadful weather, my father would be returning to England in a few days' time and so his house would be free then. He added that, if I was really desperate for shelter, I could go to the house at Caffoulens, down the road, which was empty now. I was tempted. There was little wood left, I'd just finished reading my second Brontë, and I was so miserable. And yet it would only be three days before I could move straight into my longed-for destination. Should I suffer the discomfort and misery until then and avoid the disruption of an extra move? Or should I pack up immediately and enjoy a few days in the civilized comfort of Caffoulens? I packed my bags and left.

Lacapelle

I burst into tears when I arrived at the palatial house at Caffoulens —I was so relieved to be in such comfort and within walking distance of my destination.

I spent a few happy days writing letters and being shown around the local markets by my father. Then the time came to wave goodbye to him, his wife, and their laden car, and to move myself and all my belongings into Lacapelle. I had at long last arrived where I wanted to be. I gave myself a week to settle in and complete the ritual tidying-up that must be done before I could turn once again to my writing.

I have arranged my desk so that I can look out of the window. The front balcony is covered in grapevine, green leaves, and purple grapes providing dappled shade from the sun. Across the way stand an old stone barn, a fir tree, a fig tree, and a cage of rabbits. Through the trees I can see fields sloping down towards the village of Bagnac. The old lady cleans out the rabbit hutch and Monsieur from further up the road potters around inspecting his wine barrels and prodding the bonfire. Usually it's just the dogs who keep me company. Henri, in spite of his limp and sore throat, is forever patrolling his territory. From a distance he guards the girls: an excitable collie and an ageing poodle in need of a haircut.

I can walk down to Bagnac in about fifteen minutes, though it takes longer to climb back up the steep hill. Sometimes I go down before breakfast and buy my bread and croissant.

I have an orchard rather than a garden, and when I first arrived I had to go out and gather the walnuts every day. There are apples too, but they aren't very big so I collect unwanted windfalls from other people's trees. There are masses of chestnuts around so I always take a bag with me on my walks. I can't resist picking up the fat, shiny, brown fruit. I love wandering around outside. If I'm not hunting for walnuts, I mess about with my woodpile—some of the wood is damp so I have to dry it out in the sun. I don't know what I'll do when there is no fruit of the earth to gather. Perhaps I'll do more writing!

I met my neighbour cutting down a tree in his garden. He told me to call if there was ever anything I needed. I felt pleased and re-assured that here was someone I could turn to. It was natural, alone in a foreign country, to welcome the offer of friendly help. But when I began to imagine that his wife was ignoring me out of jealousy, I decided that my little fantasies of being rescued on a dark night, when my car had broken down, and being taken into the bosom of the family, had better be knocked on the head and that I should keep to myself at all costs.

More of a Man

When the sun shines I sit outside on my balcony. The curtain of vine leaves has completely gone now and so I am exposed to my neighbours.

Next door, to my left, lives the family—mother, father, boy, girl, two dogs, and a cat. In the mornings they all set off for work and school. They come home for lunch and return again in the evening. They have two cars. Madame takes the children and Monsieur drives alone. Sometimes I see Madame in the garden hanging up the washing. Monsieur is often outside with his chain-saw or lawn-mower.

Across the road, next to the old barn that blocks most of my view down the hillside towards Bagnac, live the old couple. She steps out every day to feed the rabbits and pigeons. She wears a pinny to protect her clothes as she busies about her work. He shuffles out of the house, often just to see what's going on. Several times over the last two days I have seen him walk across to take a look at the big green plastic dustbin that was recently deposited on our 'hamlet green'. He isn't as friendly as his wife and seems to regard me with some suspicion. Sometimes he brings out his sickle and cuts a bit of grass for the rabbits. Most days he wanders off for a long walk. Coming across him on my own walks sometimes, I have been surprised at how far he has ventured from home. On Sunday they go to church, he drives, she takes charge of the shopping, and the family comes to lunch.

To my right, in the rather grand house at the very summit of our hill, live the middle-aged couple. He must be retired but he is always on the go. He is forever outside busy with something—building a wall, retiling a roof, driving off on his tractor. He argues with the old man, and his wife makes the peace. I believe she is a schoolteacher. She occasionally passes by when she visits the old couple—they might even be her parents.

As I watch from my balcony I find that it is the men I am interested in. I've taken the children to school, hung out the washing, and rejected a career. And I don't want to cook dinner for my grandchildren. I want to drive off alone. I want to be an intrepid explorer. I want to drive a tractor.

My womb has done its job, I wish it wouldn't bother me any more. I never did manage to welcome the bloody business of menstruation as one of Women's Mysteries. Without encouraging the growth of hair on my chest and my chin, I want to be more of a man.

Breakdown

The grass in the orchard grows quickly. Occasionally Robert comes to cut it. I give him a cup of tea and we talk about French country living, why he moved to France, and Buddhism.

One market day morning my car wouldn't start. The imagined breakdown had finally happened, though not, as I'd dreaded, on a dark night and far from home. Even so, I still needed help. I'd already disqualified my neighbour, so I thought of phoning Robert—it was either him or the flirtatious Monsieur T at Caffoulens.

I didn't really want to trouble either of them, and after my initial panic I realized I could manage perfectly well myself. It wasn't just a man I needed; it was a garage mechanic. I tightened my braces, pulled up my socks, armed myself with the French for timing and spark plugs, and set off for a long trek down the hill and into the as yet unexplored territory to the south of Bagnac.

All went well at the garage and I was assured that someone would be with me by the end of the morning. I bought a few vegetables at the market and struggled back up the hill in the uncomfortably hot sun. But the most difficult part of my little adventure was plucking up the courage to make a telephone call when, after two days, no one had turned up.

The car needed a new battery; then I took it down to have the timing adjusted and a faulty light fixed. They forgot to mend the light so I did it myself.

Time to Call it a Day

Away in France I still didn't feel completely happy about a life of celibacy. I wasn't beset with sexual fantasies or uncontrollable urges, but I did sometimes experience a longing for the particular intimacy I was giving up, and then I would naturally feel disappointed that it no longer lay within my reach. Nevertheless, I was prepared for a state of contentment to take time to mature and I felt fortunate to have a whole year ahead of me. I felt sure that by the end of the year my perspective would have changed dramatically and I should then be realizing the benefits of renunciation to a degree I'd not experienced before.

I had intended to remain pretty much on my own for the year, with just one or two visits from friends. I had initially assumed, a little regretfully, that I would not be seeing Subhuti. However, while on our working holiday the previous year he had suggested that if we could remain chaste he might visit me. He was particularly interested to see how I got on with my writing. I was delighted by the prospect of his company and I was sure I would appreciate any help, encouragement, sympathy, even criticism, he could offer me regarding my writing.

I'd been in France for about three months and had only recently arrived at the house I was to live in for the rest of my stay. Having been very unsettled I hadn't made much headway in my attempts to write. Now, if I wanted to have something to show to Subhuti, I simply had to get on with it.

I drove down to Toulouse to meet him from the airport. I was a little nervous about how I should greet him. Should we keep each other at arm's length? There he was, coming through the glass door. After a moment's hesitation we gave each other a warm hug. We sat down for a cup of coffee—I wasn't ready to drive straight back again. In spite of having been alone for some time I was immediately at ease in his company. It was so nice to have him beside me again and I felt quite capable of behaving myself.

Neither of us had actually taken a vow, but it didn't occur to me that we might succumb to temptation. As we sat on the sofa by the log fire Subhuti confessed the thought that he had not been able to shake from his mind. It had all been so clear, and suddenly it wasn't. He didn't actually suggest we indulge, but the flesh was weak and willing—so we did.

Had I fooled myself into thinking I really was on my way to giving up sex, I began to wonder. Now we had to work out a new plan for the rest of our time together. I felt thoroughly confused. Perhaps sex would have to remain a peripheral element to our relationship—like saying hallo and goodbye. We agreed that for this time, at least, that's how it would be. And then we turned our minds to the future. We had both found that whilst there was some unclarity or ambiguity as to whether or not we were going to pay heed to Eros, unfailingly an element of polarization would figure in our communication. We couldn't ignore the fact that we were different—he was a man and I was a woman—and as such designed to be sexually attracted to one another. It was hard to avoid just a little indulgence in the game of maintaining, even exaggerating, our differences in order to encourage desire. However, when it was quite clear that Eros was banned, our communication was more deeply satisfying and left no lingering trace of longing. We had been prevaricating too long. We had both made up our minds that we wanted to be celibate, and so, Subhuti suggested, why not start now? He had come to the conclusion that for himself that was the only way—to stop leaving loopholes and putting himself in tantalizing situations. I felt myself tightening up, resisting, but all I could do was agree. And then slowly, as we talked on, I experienced a sense of relief. Yes, that really was what I wanted too. And just think, he said, we won't ever have to have one of these agonizing conversations again.

He wanted to go a step further—he wanted to become an *anagarika*.

Alone in France I had watched my fantasies and reflected on my desire to be looked after and protected. I had come to the conclusion that I was quite capable of fending for myself, that I didn't need, and rarely wanted, to be looked after, and that, although I too hated shopping, I did—unlike my reluctant daughter—want to be responsible. My knight had served me well and now it was time for him to go free, and for me to stand firmly on my own two feet. His shining armour would turn to saffron cloth, and I must become more of a man.

An experiment had failed. I had known it wouldn't prove easy but I had so wanted it to work. I so enjoyed spending a few days at a time in Subhuti's company. But perhaps, I thought, I should rejoice in what we had enjoyed rather than bemoan what was not to be in the future. It was obviously not wise for us to consider spending a night together under the same roof. I had half hoped, earlier on, that Subhuti might come and visit me again. It would now be out of the question. Not necessarily, he said. Perhaps he could come but stay at Caffoulens, up the road. We decided to wait until nearer the time, to see whether it would be possible and whether we both still considered it a good idea.

We played 'our song'—the music from our first encounter. And then we said goodbye.

A Knight Unto Myself

Early in the morning I drove Subhuti down to Bagnac station. As I returned up the hill to be on my own once more, I felt a sense of loss, but I was convinced we had done the right thing. Back at Lacapelle I took a vow of celibacy to seal my conviction.

For several days my life was tranquil, and then the inevitable reaction set in. I had been reading George Eliot's *Mill on the Floss* and when, at the end, brother and sister died in each other's arms, I wept and wept. I could no longer concentrate on my writing. I felt lonely and empty. I felt angry. I wanted to be angry with Subhuti. I wanted to be unreasonable. But how could I? I had never had cause to be angry with him before and neither had I now.

I latched all my fears on to the idea of his becoming an *anagarika*. But why should I dread it? Because it was so final? What would it mean in practice, I wondered. Could I still touch him? Would I still be special to him? Would we be very guarded in our behaviour towards one another? Ought I to keep out of his way? I desperately wanted to talk to him again before he took such a step. I had no intention of trying to dissuade him from it—at least not con-sciously—I just wanted to discuss my worries whilst he could still put his arm around me and reassure me. How painful it had been to hold back from Sona when he and I were disentangling ourselves from one another. I didn't want to go through that again. I knew that we would each have our own personal struggles. He had asked me to help him. What would that entail? Would I help him by keeping away from him, by discouraging him from coming to see me just when I so dear-ly wanted him near me again? Oh! if only my own vision of the angelic life were more vivid and alluring....

He wrote from India to say that he would be becoming an *anagarika* in a couple of weeks' time whilst there. I felt as though struck by a thunderbolt. I hadn't imagined that there would be no occasion to talk before he publicly took the monk's life upon himself. He asked for my blessing. I felt deeply sorry and ashamed that I couldn't im-mediately give it. It took me twenty-four hours to get over the shock and stop feeling sorry for myself, before I could begin to feel pleased on his account. Over the following days I felt calmer and happier and I really did feel very glad that at long last he was taking a step that meant so much to him. I even experienced a sense of freedom and clarity in myself, and I realized I was no longer in conflict. I had stopped worrying about how much time I would get to spend with him and whether or not I could touch him. I just thought of him and rejoiced. I was glad that he'd gone ahead and become an *anagarika* before I'd had a chance to confess my fears. I had to face them alone.

I had to face the deep desire to remain attached, bound, limited, imprisoned. I had to face the pain that attachment engenders. No matter how chivalrous had been my knight, I had to come to my own rescue. I had to be a knight unto myself and I discovered that my own two feet were dependable after all.

I had been prepared for Subhuti not to come and see me again. As far as my writing went I wasn't sure I had much to show him after all. But I couldn't deny that I wanted him to come and I was so very pleased when he said he also wanted to. He was determined that the end of one aspect of our relationship should not mean that we could no longer be friends. He was determined to prove that it could only make a difference for the better. He wanted to show me that in becoming an *anagarika* he would not withhold his feelings of affection for me.

We spent a very enjoyable and uncomplicated few days together. I had come to a full stop with my writing and his encouragement, appreciation, and constructive comments were exactly what I needed to help me to re-engage. And his delightful, energetic, and relaxed company was exactly what I needed to see that, although he was now committed to a life of celibacy, we could remain affectionate friends.

My own thoughts on becoming an *anagarika* were revived. It seemed to me that my attraction to such a life, although sincere, had been too vague, and that I had been waiting for my perspective to change before I could contemplate it in earnest. I had needed to give up sex before I could resolve my resistance to doing so. I had needed a deeper appreciation and experience of positive aloneness. Living in France, in spite of the tough times, had given me that. It was clear to me now that I wanted to deepen that experience and that I was indeed inspired to become an *anagarika*. My vision was no longer blurred, and I could distinctly hear the angels calling.

I will have to wait, though, just a little bit longer. I have just a little bit more mothering to do. Shanti and Sundari say they have been saving up their illnesses for me so that I can look after them on my return!

Crossing Over

One of my walks led me down a steep, winding path, through the trees dropping acorns and chestnuts, to a grassy glade by a shallow, fast-flowing river. The path ended at the river's edge, and for those on horseback it re-emerged on the other side. There was, though, another way to cross. About six feet above the water, a narrow log lay stretched from bank to bank; it bore metal plates to guide the feet, and a loose wire, a balancing aid, hung alongside. I was tempted to try to cross, but in the aftermath of rain the river flowed furiously and I imagined being thrown off balance by the turbulence beneath me.

I took Subhuti down to the river. He saw the bridge and, before I'd had time to say perhaps we wouldn't go that way, he was striding across. I stood at the edge of the bank and looked down at the water. I took hold of the wire; it was too loose to steady me if I should lose my balance. Subhuti warned me that the metal plates wobbled a bit. I tentatively put one foot forward and my legs turned to jelly. As he encouraged me on I felt my heart quivering and I knew I couldn't do it. I wandered off along the riverside, hoping to calm down so that I could try afresh. But I couldn't stop trembling, and reluctantly I admitted defeat. I felt upset. My vulnerability had let me down and I'd prevented Subhuti from exploring further. He said he was sure I would do it one day. I wasn't so sure.

Alone again, my walks occasionally led me down to the river. I stood on the first foot-pad and felt a little dizzy. Disappointed, I stepped back. On my third visit I was determined that the fast-flowing water shouldn't mesmerize me. I took a couple of steps forward and found I could maintain my balance. I considered carrying on, but just in case I did fall I thought it would be more sensible to wait until I had company. I felt excited, looking forward now to the day when I would cross over.

Several days later I found myself walking down towards the river. I kept telling myself that I wasn't going to try to cross but I knew that I wanted to. I stood for a little while at the edge of the log. I took a couple of steps forward, and then another, and then standing poised over the river I knew I'd gone too far to turn back. My knees went weak and my heart thumped as I nervously carried on my way. But I did it! I crossed to the other side. I was so pleased with myself.

The path ahead was the most delightful I'd yet come across. It wound its way close to the river for some distance and then led up through the wooded hillside. There I turned round, having calmed down enough to contemplate the return crossing.

If any incident could be described as symbolic of my year away, it was this. Overcoming my vulnerability, my aspiration conquered my weak flesh. Leaving behind the familiar shore, I stepped forward on my own to explore the land that lay beyond. If I wanted to continue to explore, I must be prepared to cross over time and time again.

Geraniums

In late April flower stalls appeared at the market. I was tempted by the bright colours. Out on my walks I loved seeing balconies decorated with pots of flowers—usually red geraniums. I'd had a geranium in my sitting-room in Norwich; it was the most wonderful, vibrant pink colour. I looked for one that most nearly resembled it, and bought it as a token gesture.

My balcony had been looking rather bare with the grapevine not yet in leaf. It was soon cheered up by the pink geranium. But then the geranium looked rather lonely. My eyes wandered across the front of the house, and I envisaged pots of geraniums extending up the stone steps and along the whole length of the balcony—that was what I really wanted. But was it worth it, I pondered, when I'd be leaving soon? I quickly dismissed my desire as extravagant and indulgent; it was that crafty Mara, I decided, tempting me to put down my roots, to become attached, and make this my home when it was only a temporary abode.

The next week at the market I bought another pink geranium to accompany the first, and a trailing one to hang from the balcony. I still wasn't satisfied. Why shouldn't I make my temporary abode look pleasing, I asked myself. Others could enjoy them when I'd gone. I determined to put aside my reservations (which really amounted to stinginess), to be bold, and buy a few more. But by the time market day came around again, to my dismay, the geraniums were no longer at their best, and there were very few pink ones. I nearly resigned myself to those I already had but 'that's what you always do,' a little voice said. So, over the following weeks, I rooted around for healthy-looking plants.

Now, whenever I open the front door, I smile at the row of geraniums greeting me in full bloom. My balcony isn't full of them, but I'm happy with what I've got.

Time to Go

A few days ago I went for my occasional visit to the French equivalent of Sainsburys. I was attracted by the display of summer clothes. I thought I might buy some espadrilles—after all I was in France—but my toes felt too cramped in them. Then a long cotton shirt caught my eye. It was the colour of *anagarika* robes. I tried it on; it fitted perfectly. But I knew, without a moment's hesitation, that I wouldn't buy it.

I cannot hurry the step I am going to take. I am no longer running a race—my future beckons, and I am walking towards it with stillness, simplicity, contentment, and confidence. I want to leave no regrets in my wake, and I want to hear no more distracting cries of 'Mum! There's a wasp in my room!'

The first magnificent blooms of the geraniums are fading now. Their petals are shrivelling up and dropping on to the wooden floor of my balcony.... It's nearly time for me to go.... But there are lots more bright pink jewels peeping out of their green casing—lots more flowers to come.... And I'll be going back to a new life.

I am going to live in a community.

Afterword

Sundari spilt blackcurrant juice on her beautiful white dressing-gown. 'Quick, quick, Mum!' she said, 'Do something!' I suggested she soak it in cold water and maybe put salt on it. 'No, you do it,' she said. 'You're the Mum.'

It's impossible not to be otherwise. I came home from France determined not to slip back too readily into my role as mother. But Sundari, who considered that I left her alone too soon, thought I had some making up to do. I respond because I want to finish my job off well and I want us both to enjoy our last few months together. Sometimes, however, I get frustrated.

Yesterday morning I got up late. I couldn't settle to my writing and with a deadline to meet I began to worry. I asked Sundari to go into the city to buy my mother a birthday card, but she said she couldn't. I shut myself in my room feeling frustrated, upset, and resentful. Why couldn't she put herself out a bit? I'd tried so hard—or so I thought—not to be a nagging mother. We'd lived our separate lives for a year. She was glad to have me back and yet I wished she would show it by being more helpful in the house. I knew I had a point and yet I also knew I was overreacting and unreasonably blaming her for my more general frustration and unhappiness. I might have had cause for disappointment but I could not excuse my feelings of resentment. Sometimes I not only expect too much of myself, I expect it, or at least want it, of others too. Our near-arguments had become more frequent. They had been occurring when Sundari's hormones were playing havoc. She now suggested that mine might be disturbing me, and she was right. She dealt with me very well, and we're now both making more of an effort not to take our bad moods out on each other, and to be more demonstrative of our appreciation of one another.

I constantly have to remind myself that I am still in the midst of great change and I find it very unsettling. I am determined that once my present change of life is complete, the menopause will be, in comparison, insignificant. The change began with my decision to go away for a year, and it will end with my leaving home.

Before I went away to France, Bhante asked the Public Preceptors and some other senior Order members to form a sort of Council of Elders which could take over all of his remaining responsibilities, both administrative and spiritual. He wanted us to act as a unifying influence in the movement, making sure that the same standards of spiritual practice were maintained. He would then be free to do whatever he pleased, whilst keeping a watchful eye over us as we found our feet. He wanted us to live together, in communities based around a building that would serve as central offices and meeting rooms for the Order and the FWBO. A house was soon found, in Birmingham— suitable both for the general offices and a men's community. It appeared that my future was cut out for me. It was very good timing. After my year away I would be ready for a big move. I was very happy for Bhante to determine it, and if Birmingham was considered a convenient place, so be it.

I looked forward to the prospect of living and working so closely with others, but I didn't stop to imagine what it would be like to live in Birmingham. I had heard that the building already acquired was situated in a very pleasant, even rural, part of the city. Soon after returning from France, I visited with Sanghadevi, in search of a house for our new community. It was then that it struck me that, having wanted never to move back to London, I was now looking for a home in Britain's second largest city. There were parks and trees and some very fine houses to be found in the area we were concentrating on, but it was hardly rural. I felt depressed for the whole of our stay, and ashamed that my longing for community life was hardly evident under my gloomy perspective.

On my next visit the depression lifted. I was there to take part in the first full meeting of the Council, with all thirteen members present. My future was beginning to look less abstract. It was with these friends in particular that I would be working. But what exactly was our brief? I acknowledged feelings of insecurity. I was embarking on a new phase of my life, taking on a great responsibility, without knowing just what it would involve and how I would function in it, and I was still in the midst of letting go of my previous life, feeling a bit reluctant and even afraid to be moving on so definitely from mother-hood. I was interested and relieved to find that others, in their own ways had similar feelings.

The most specific brief we had had from Bhante was one that was familiar to me. He wanted us to strengthen our friendships and learn to work harmoniously together. In a way, he said, everything would flow from that. Remembering this I felt encouraged. I was already in the company of some very good friends: Devamitra and Sanghadevi, with whom I had enjoyed long-standing working relationships; and Sona and Subhuti, with whom I had emerged triumphant from long-standing romantic attachment; and Sinhadevi would soon be living with me.

My story ends as I embark on my new life—a time I have looked forward to for so long. But my struggles, I know, will continue, for although I will have literally left home, having made some progress in weakening attachment, there is still a long way to go before I find real freedom.

Shanti and Sundari aren't very happy that I am not intending to stay long at Lollard's Road providing a family home for them. In the Buddha's day, when a woman went forth from home, she would first need to obtain permission from her husband or her father. I hope that when the time comes my daughters will give me their blessings.

GLOSSARY

AMBEDKAR, DR B.R. An ex-Untouchable who had the rare opportunity of a Western education, Dr Ambedkar was independent India's first Law Minister. Sangharakshita knew him personally, and played an important part in the 'Mass Conversion Movement' that Ambedkar set in motion.

ANAGARIKA This traditional term literally means 'homeless one'. In the Western Buddhist Order there is no monastic ordination, but some Order members do undertake to observe a vow of chastity—observing *brahmacharya* (q.v.)—for an extended period as an aspect of their spiritual practice.

BHANTE Literally meaning 'teacher', this is a respectful and affectionate term used to address Sangharakshita.

BHIKKHU A Buddhist monk (*bhikkhuni* means 'nun'); traditionally a wandering mendicant who begs for his food and teaches the Dharma (q.v.).

BODHISATTVA Literally an 'Enlightenment being', the Bodhisattva undertakes to gain Enlightenment not just for their own sake but for the sake of all beings.

BRAHMACHARYA A Sanskrit word, normally translated as 'chastity', but implying far more than mere abstention from sexual activity. It is to live less and less bound by the senses, and by the possessions and securities of the material world. One who observes *brahmacharya* finds an increasingly deep source of happiness and fulfilment in spiritual friendship, meditation, and devotion.

DHARMA A word with numerous meanings. It can mean 'truth' or 'reality'; it is also used to refer to all those teachings and methods that are conducive to gaining Enlightenment.

DHARMACHARI (m.)/DHARMACHARINI (f.) Meaning 'Dharma-farer' or 'practitioner of the Dharma'. The term goes back to the Buddha, being found in the *Dhammapada*:

> The *Dhammacari* lives happily, (both) in this
> world and the world beyond.

This title, given at ordination, emphasizes the Western Buddhist Order's link with essential Buddhist tradition.

GOING FOR REFUGE Going for Refuge to the Three Jewels (q.v.) is the act of committing oneself to gaining Enlightenment, and this is what the phrase usually refers to. Sangharakshita has said that Going for Refuge is the 'central and definitive act of the Buddhist life' and 'the unifying principle, therefore, of Buddhism itself'.

GOING FORTH The act of leaving behind 'false refuges'—such as sexual relationships and a career as an end in itself—in order to direct our energies more towards the transcendental. The archetypal Going Forth was that of the Buddha, who went forth from his family and material wealth in order to seek the truth.

KALYANA MITRATA *Mitrata* means 'friendship' and *kalayana* means 'beautiful, charming, auspicious, helpful, morally good'. True spiritual friendship, or *kalyana mitrata*, gives one access to those higher spiritual experiences that provide a basis of inspiration and confidence to move forward on the path.

MAHAYANA Literally the 'great way'. Those schools of Buddhism that emphasize the Bodhisattva (q.v.) Ideal.

MANDALA It can be helpful to think in terms of having a 'personal mandala'. At the centre is whatever is most important in one's life, and around it—in the circle of the mandala—are arranged all one's other interests and preoccupations.

MARA In traditional Buddhism, Mara is seen as the personification of all our weaknesses, the tempter who tries to undermine our spiritual efforts.

PURE LAND According to Mahayana Buddhism, this is a realm in which conditions are totally favourable to progress towards Buddhahood. A Pure Land can therefore be considered to be an archetype of the perfect society.

SANGHA As one of the Three Jewels (q.v.) it refers to the Arya or Noble Sangha —those Buddhist practitioners who have gained insight into the true nature of things and whose progress towards Buddhahood is certain. In the widest sense, the Sangha is the community of all those who are following the path to Enlightenment.

STREAM ENTRY According to Hinayana Buddhism, the Stream Entrant is someone who, in breaking the Three Fetters (q.v.), has developed a degree of transcendental insight. Once one has gained Stream Entry, progress towards the goal of full Enlightenment is irreversible.

STUPA Originally the stupa was a mound or structure built to commemorate a Buddha, and it often contained relics. It became a highly visible symbol of Enlightenment which assumed various architectural forms in many different countries.

SUTRA (Pali: SUTTA) A discourse given by the Buddha, or by one of his senior disciples and approved by him.

TEAM-BASED RIGHT LIVELIHOOD BUSINESSES Right Livelihood is the traditional Buddhist term for work which is ethical and helpful to spiritual development. The function of team-based Right Livelihood ventures is to provide workers in the business with their material needs, a situation within which they can experience spiritual friendship, and to make a profit that can be given to the Buddhist centre with which the business is connected, or to some other cause.

TEN PRECEPTS, At ordination, members of the Western Buddhist Order undertake a traditional list of ten precepts which offer a fundamental code of ethical conduct, including body, speech, and mind.

THREE FETTERS, These are 'fixed self-view', 'doubt' or lack of commitment, and 'dependence on mere morality or religious observances as ends in themselves'. The breaking of these fetters (the first three of ten) is synonymous with Stream Entry (q.v.).

THREE JEWELS, These are the traditional symbols for the Buddha, Dharma, and Sangha, to which a Buddhist goes for Refuge (q.v.).

The Windhorse symbolizes the energy of the enlightened mind carrying the Three Jewels—the Buddha, the Dharma, and the Sangha—to all sentient beings.

Buddhism is one of the fastest growing spiritual traditions in the Western world.

Throughout its 2,500-year history, it has always succeeded in adapting its mode of expression to suit whatever culture it has encountered. Windhorse Publications aims to continue this tradition as Buddhism comes to the West. Today's Westerners are heirs to the entire Buddhist tradition, free to draw instruction and inspiration from all the many schools and branches. Windhorse publishes works by authors who not only understand the Buddhist tradition but are also familiar with Western culture and the Western mind.

For orders and catalogues contact

WINDHORSE PUBLICATIONS
UNIT 1-316
THE CUSTARD FACTORY
GIBB STREET
BIRMINGHAM
B9 4AA
UK

WINDHORSE PUBLICATIONS (USA)
14 HEARTWOOD CIRCLE
NEWMARKET
NEW HAMPSHIRE
NH 03857
USA

Windhorse Publications is an arm of the Friends of the Western Buddhist Order, which has more than sixty centres on four continents. Through these centres, members of the Western Buddhist Order offer regular programmes of events for the general public and for more experienced students. These include meditation classes, public talks, study on Buddhist themes and texts, and 'bodywork' classes such as T'ai Chi Chu'an, yoga, and massage. The FWBO also runs several retreat centres and the Karuna Trust, a fundraising charity that supports social welfare projects in the slums and villages of India.

Many FWBO centres have residential spiritual communities and ethical businesses associated with them. Arts activities are encouraged too, as is the development of strong bonds of friendship between people who share the same ideals. In this way the FWBO is developing a unique approach to Buddhism, not simply as a set of techniques, less still as an exotic cultural interest, but as a creatively directed way of life for people living in the modern world.

If you would like more information about the FWBO please write to

LONDON BUDDHIST CENTRE
51 ROMAN ROAD
LONDON
E2 0HU
UK

ARYALOKA
HEARTWOOD CIRCLE
NEWMARKET
NEW HAMPSHIRE
NH 03857
USA

Also From Windhorse

SUBHUTI
Bringing Buddhism to the West: A Life of Sangharakshita
Born in London, Dennis Lingwood realized that he was a Buddhist at the age of sixteen. Conscripted during the Second World War, army life took him to India where he stayed on to become the Buddhist monk Sangharakshita. By the mid-fifties he was an increasingly active and forthright exponent of Buddhism, and had established a uniquely non-sectarian centre in Kalimpong.

As hippies flocked eastwards in the sixties, Sangharakshita returned to England to establish the Friends of the Western Buddhist Order. This movement has been pioneering a vital form of Buddhism for the modern world. It is also at the heart of a Buddhist revival in India—the land where Buddhism was born 2,500 years ago.

Sangharakshita's story is proof that it is possible to live a truly spiritual life in the modern world.

208 pages plus 12 pages of photographs, index
ISBN 0 904766 69 1
£9.99 / $18.95

SANGHARAKSHITA
Buddhism for Today - and Tomorrow
To lead a Buddhist life we need, above all, four things: a vision of the kind of person we could become; practical methods to help us transform ourselves in the light of that vision; friendship to support and encourage us on the path; and a society or culture that supports us in our aspirations.

This book is a succinct introduction to a Buddhist movement that exists precisely to make these things available. Sangharakshita brought the experience of twenty years' practice of Buddhism in India back to his native Britain, to found the Friends of the Western Buddhist Order in 1967.

This heartfelt statement of his vision is recommended reading for anyone who aspires to live a Buddhist life in the world today—and tomorrow.

64 pages
Recommended reading list and index
ISBN 0 904766 83 7
£4.99 / $8.95